Cambridge Elements ≡

Elements in Public Policy
edited by
M. Ramesh
National University of Singapore
Michael Howlett
Simon Fraser University, British Columbia
Xun Wu
Hong Kong University of Science and Technology
Judith Clifton
University of Cantabria
Eduardo Araral
National University of Singapore

POLICY ENTREPRENEURS AND DYNAMIC CHANGE

Michael Mintrom
Monash University

CAMBRIDGE
UNIVERSITY PRESS

CAMBRIDGE
UNIVERSITY PRESS

University Printing House, Cambridge CB2 8BS, United Kingdom

One Liberty Plaza, 20th Floor, New York, NY 10006, USA

477 Williamstown Road, Port Melbourne, VIC 3207, Australia

314–321, 3rd Floor, Plot 3, Splendor Forum, Jasola District Centre,
New Delhi – 110025, India

79 Anson Road, #06–04/06, Singapore 079906

Cambridge University Press is part of the University of Cambridge.

It furthers the University's mission by disseminating knowledge in the pursuit of
education, learning, and research at the highest international levels of excellence.

www.cambridge.org
Information on this title: www.cambridge.org/9781108461467
DOI: 10.1017/9781108605946

© Michael Mintrom 2020

First published 2020

A catalogue record for this publication is available from the British Library.

ISBN 978-1-108-46146-7 Paperback
ISSN 2398-4058 (online)
ISSN 2514-3565 (print)

Policy Entrepreneurs and Dynamic Change

Elements in Public Policy

DOI: 10.1017/9781108605946
First published online: October 2019

Michael Mintrom
Monash University
Author for correspondence: Michael Mintrom, michael.mintrom@monash.edu

Abstract: Policy entrepreneurs are energetic actors who engage in collaborative efforts in and around government to promote policy innovations. Interest in policy entrepreneurs has grown over recent years. Increasingly, they are recognized as a unique class of political actors, who display common attributes, deploy common strategies and can propel dynamic shifts in societal practices. This Element assesses the current state of knowledge on policy entrepreneurs, their actions and their impacts. It explains how various global forces are creating new demand for policy entrepreneurship, and suggests directions for future research on policy entrepreneurs and their efforts to drive dynamic change.

Keywords: advocacy coalitions; policy entrepreneurs; problem framing; policy innovation; policymaking

ISBNs: 9781108461467 (PB), 9781108605946 (OC)
ISSNs: 2398-4058 (online), 2514-3565 (print)

Contents

When people make a fundamental choice to be true to what is highest in them, or when they make a choice to fulfil a purpose in their life, they can easily accomplish many changes that seemed impossible or improbable in the past.

Robert Fritz

1 Policy Entrepreneurs as Change Agents

Policy entrepreneurs are energetic actors who work with others in and around policymaking venues to promote policy innovations. Over recent decades, interest in policy entrepreneurs has grown exponentially. That interest has come both from scholars of public policy and from individuals working in and around government. Scholars of public policy have sought to better understand the roles that policy entrepreneurs play in policymaking processes. Their key concerns have been how and why policy entrepreneurs matter (Anderson, DeLeo and Taylor 2019; Frisch-Aviram, Cohen and Beeri 2019; Narbutaite Aflaki, Miles and Petridou 2015; Mintrom and Norman 2009). For practitioners, the key concern has been how they might improve their own practice. They have looked to lessons drawn from the study of policy entrepreneurs to improve how they formulate and advance specific policy positions (Kalil 2017; Mintrom 2003).

This Element reviews our current knowledge of policy entrepreneurs as change agents. It is intended to contribute both to scholarship and practice. For scholars of public policy, this Element indicates fruitful areas for future research and suggests effective methods for pursuing such research. For practitioners, this Element catalogues common dispositions and strategies of policy entrepreneurs. For those working in and around government, that knowledge should prove beneficial both to those starting their careers and those moving into leadership positions. Much can be learned about policy formulation and effective ways to drive policy change through reflecting on specific cases of policy entrepreneurship.

As they work to promote significant policy change, policy entrepreneurs exhibit well-documented regularities both in their personal dispositions and in the strategies they deploy. Policy entrepreneurs are ambitious in pursuit of a cause. They display sociability and exhibit high levels of social acuity. To secure credibility within specific policy circles, they draw on their past accomplishments and expertise, their professional connections and whatever power or prestige they enjoy in their current positions. They are tenacious. In promoting significant policy change, policy entrepreneurs deploy several strategies. These include framing problems and redefining policy solutions, using and expanding networks, creating advocacy teams and coalitions, leading by example and scaling-up advocacy initiatives to expand the scope of policy change. Yet, even as they frequently conform to these observed regularities of disposition and strategy, policy entrepreneurs display diversity in their policy interests, where they operate and how they engage in advocacy activities.

1.1 Entrepreneurs in Business, Society and Politics

Entrepreneurs have been viewed for centuries as crucial societal actors who develop and bring new products and services to market. Through their actions, entrepreneurs often catalyse new forms of economic and social activity (Casson 1982; Kirzner 1997; Schumpeter 1934). Often, entrepreneurs in the marketplace face strong competition. Existing producers, perceiving threats to their business, can make it hard for new players to succeed with their ventures. However, when entrepreneurs meet with success, their actions can generate dynamic change. Think, for example, of how technological advances have made it easier for people to purchase a vast array of products and services from their phones. As increasing numbers of consumers access new products and services, it is inevitable that those producers who make no changes to how they engage with customers are likely to confront shrinking demand. Such dynamic changes in markets signal shifts from status quo business activities. Entrepreneurs distinguish themselves from run-of-the-mill business owners because they exhibit a desire to do things differently. While many people in business will be satisfied to build up their businesses in established markets, entrepreneurs take calculated risks in the hope of opening up new profit opportunities.

In the past few decades, while endeavours have continued to improve our knowledge of entrepreneurs and market processes, efforts have also been made to identify and describe entrepreneurial actors elsewhere in society (Battilana, Leca and Boxenbaum 2009; Bornstein and Davis 2010; Narbutaite Aflaki, Miles and Petridou 2015). The claim driving these newer explorations is that those who promote innovation in the world of politics, in policymaking processes and within specific institutions and organizations frequently resemble entrepreneurs in the marketplace (Kingdon 1984 [2011]; Mintrom 2000; Sheingate 2003). Indeed, common dispositions and actions can be found across entrepreneurial actors, no matter whether they are operating in market settings, political and governmental settings, or social and community settings.

Policy entrepreneurs play a unique role in policymaking processes. They represent a class of political actor distinguished by their attempts to introduce and drive proposals for policy innovation. Often, in promoting such innovations, policy entrepreneurs display a willingness to form alliances and cross institutional and organizational boundaries in ways rarely seen among other political actors. The figure of the policy entrepreneur was introduced to the public policy literature by John W. Kingdon in his book *Agenda, Alternatives, and Public Policies*. Kingdon said policy entrepreneurs 'could be in or out of government, in elected or appointed positions, in interest groups or research organizations. But their defining characteristic, much as in the case of the business entrepreneur, is their willingness to invest their resources – time, energy, reputation, and sometimes money – in the hope of a future return' (1984 [2011], p. 122). Following Kingdon, many scholars have sought to further define and systematically study common attributes of policy entrepreneurs, the actions they take and the degree of success they meet in championing policy innovations.

In studying policy entrepreneurs, we should be concerned that all forms of political action will be viewed as approximations of policy entrepreneurship. We should also be concerned that all forms of policy change may be labelled as policy innovations. To overcome these concerns, boundaries must be established around both the concept of the policy entrepreneur and the concept of policy innovation. I will return to this matter later in this section.

1.2 Four Policy Entrepreneurs

Before going further in our exploration of policy entrepreneurs, it is useful to get a sense of what these actors are like, and the kinds of policy changes they introduce. To that end, this section offers brief portraits of four policy entrepreneurs. Each are extraordinary individuals who created major policy legacies. They had significant and ongoing impacts on the practices of many other people. The four are: Ken Livingstone, a former mayor of London; Bob Klein, a California property developer, William Hague, a former British foreign secretary, and Aloisea Inyumba, a former Rwandan minister for gender and family promotion. Many others – heralding from a broad range of positions inside and outside of government – have acted over recent decades as policy entrepreneurs. These four are representative in the sense that they come from diverse contexts and each pursued matters of considerable importance.

Ken Livingstone and Climate Change Action

The C40 Cities Climate Leadership Group is composed of mayors from the world's largest cities who are committed to reducing greenhouse gas emissions. The group was originally convened by Ken Livingstone. As mayor of London from 2000 to 2008, Livingstone aimed to position London as a leading global city. The London Plan, officially launched in 2004, distilled Livingstone's desire to make London a green city (Acuto, 2013). Under his Climate Change Action Plan, he called for London to get 25 per cent of its power from more efficient local sources and reduce carbon emissions by 60 per cent within twenty years. He pledged significant resources to these efforts. Livingstone has said climate change, and how to avert it, consumes him. It informed his mayoral decisions on transport, social housing and new business developments.

In 2005, Livingstone hosted the World Cities Leadership and Climate Summit in London. Representatives from eighteen large cities visited London to discuss actions they could take to reduce greenhouse gas emissions. Livingstone represented cities as central agents in the response to climate change (Dudley 2013). Until this point, governments of nation-states were expected to take the lead on addressing climate change. As the symbolic 'voice of London', Livingstone emphasized that cities consume over two-thirds of the world's energy and account for more than 70 per cent of global carbon dioxide emissions. Cities are also extremely vulnerable to climate change, as 75 per cent of urban settlements are at risk from sea-level rise (McGranahan, Balk and Anderson 2007).

In establishing C40, Livingstone argued that cities should take 'practical action on the ground' and not fuss with brand new approaches to sustainability (Acuto, 2013). Livingstone sought to learn from the actions of cities around the world that were using innovative means to reduce their emissions. By focusing on building requirements, insulation, solid waste, energy efficiency, traffic congestion and water systems, Livingstone suggested the group could have an immediate impact on greenhouse gas emissions.

Upon conclusion of the 2005 summit, the eighteen cities formed the C20 Partnership and issued a joint communique that committed to holding a follow-up meeting to measure progress and to report back to the United Nations (UN). Negotiating the establishment of this group initially meant the formalization of existing ties among major cities. The partnership quickly grew to comprise forty members and, under Livingstone's leadership, the group installed a London-based secretariat, appointed a steering committee, and introduced an issue-specific workshop programme.

In 2006, the group partnered with the William J. Clinton Foundation to use the newly created Clinton Climate Initiative (CCI) to implement C40 initiatives. This partnership resulted in a set of collaborative subnetworks. CCI also developed a database of member city jurisdictional capacities and actions to create a platform for intercity sharing of ideas, information and data. Through partnerships and collaboration, C40 increased its ability to leverage the potential for intercity transfer of knowledge to drive local changes (Schreurs 2008). C40's reach and influence has continued to grow. In recent times, it has formed partnerships with the World Bank, Bloomberg Philanthropies, World Resources Institute (WRI) and Local Governments for Sustainability (ICLEI).

C40's collaborations with WRI and ICLEI produced a global guide for accounting and reporting community-scale greenhouse gas emissions that can be used across multiple platforms. This was the first internationally accepted framework for city-level greenhouse gas inventories. For more discussion of this case, see Mintrom and Luetjens (2017).

Bob Klein and the Funding of Stem Cell Research

Stem cell research promises to contribute significantly to the quality of human life. However, funding of that research has often met with controversy. In 2002, California became the first state in the United States to pass legislation that explicitly allowed stem cell research involving both the destruction and donation of human embryos. The bill was intended to bolster the attractiveness of California as a location for stem cell researchers. No new funding was associated with passage of this law. The subsequent political action that opened up major funding streams for stem cell research in California revolved around the drafting and approval of a citizen proposition, Proposition 71, the California Stem Cell Research and Cures Act of 2004.

The move to secure extensive support for stem cell research in California was spearheaded by Bob Klein. Klein, a multimillionaire and graduate of the Stanford Law School at Stanford University, made his fortune through the development of state-funded low-income housing in California. During his career, he gained extensive experience engaging in quiet actions to secure political support for property development activities. Significantly, one of Bob Klein's sons suffers from autoimmune-mediated (type 1) diabetes. Klein noted this as a primary motivator for his advocacy of stem cell research.

Proposition 71 was designed to amend the state constitution to further facilitate embryonic stem cell research. The proposition also established the California Institute for Regenerative Medicine (CIRM) – the state stem cell agency – and authorized a bond sale to allow around US$300 million per year for embryonic stem cell research over a ten-year period. That level of expenditure represented significantly more than what the federal government was committing to stem cell research at the time. Indeed, it exceeded the funding for this research provided by any other jurisdiction in the world.

In developing and promoting Proposition 71, Bob Klein took great care to emphasize the creation of cures for degenerative diseases. Thus, the proposition was named 'the California Stem Cell Research and Cures Act'. Bob Klein worked closely with venture capitalists, leaders of biotechnology firms and representatives of the state's strong scientific and medical research communities while drafting the proposition. The proposition bypassed the legislative process, eliminating the need for compromise in the enacting legislation. It funded stem cell research through bond issues, which protected it from subsequent cutbacks due to fiscal constraint.

Klein chaired the 'Yes on 71' campaign. Throughout the campaign, he made powerful arguments to state political leaders and citizens alike that funding for stem cell research promised major pay offs for California. These pay offs were presented as the saving of lives through scientific advancement and the securing of greater economic prosperity through the expansion of high-technology industries. California's Proposition 71 passed with support from a strong majority of voters. Klein subsequently served as chair of the Independent Citizens Oversight Committee that governs the CIRM. From there, he went on to serve two terms as chair of the CIRM governing board. Today, CIRM is a thriving enterprise with ambitious goals for the future. It is a global leader in supporting stem cell research. For more discussion of this case, see Mintrom (2015).

William Hague and the Preventing Sexual Violence Initiative

Sexual violence during war and conflict is not a new phenomenon. However, its use in contemporary war and conflict appears to have increased. Since the mass rapes that took place in Bosnia–Herzegovina and Rwanda in the 1990s, widespread, systematic use of sexual violence has been documented in many conflicts. In 2000, the UN Security Council adopted its first resolution on Women, Peace and Security. Resolution 1325 recognized the impact of armed conflict on women and girls. In 2010, the UN Security Council adopted Resolution 1960. This called for detailed reporting within the UN on situations and perpetrators of sexual violence, to be monitored by the special representative on sexual violence in armed conflict.

As British foreign secretary (2010–14), William Hague incorporated international recognition and implementation of Resolution 1325 into the daily functions of the Foreign and Commonwealth Office (FCO). Hague framed sexual violence as a problem that could be addressed through his foreign policymaking. While visiting conflict zones as shadow foreign secretary, Hague came to view sexual violence in conflict as a significant concern for the UK government.

Once ensconced as foreign secretary, Hague mobilized the UK government and the international community around his Preventing Sexual Violence in Conflict Initiative, which he launched in 2012. The launch took place at a screening of Angelina Jolie's film *In the Land of Blood and Honey*. As well as being an American actress, Jolie was at the time special envoy of the UN high commissioner for refugees. Launching the initiative, Hague described his shock that only thirty individuals had been prosecuted, given that at least 50,000 rape crimes were committed during the Bosnian War. He said the initiative was central to his foreign policy goals and to the pursuit of international peace and security.

Hague's actions set in motion three streams of activity. First, a UK team of experts was created to be deployed to armed conflict areas to prevent and respond to sexual violence. Second, Hague's initiative was integrated across the work of the FCO to inform all diplomatic relationships. Third, a diplomatic campaign on preventing sexual violence in conflict was rolled out. As a prelude to Britain's presidency of the G8 in 2013, Hague deliberately built momentum around the initiative. Such summits were generally focused on the global economy and traditional barriers to growth and prosperity. Placing the issue of sexual violence as a threat to international peace and security on the G8 Summit agenda was unprecedented. However, with his novel framing and personal embrace of the issue, Hague was able to generate a statement of commitment from G8 leaders to ending sexual violence in conflict. Since 2012, over £20 million have been allocated to the initiative. For more discussion of this case, see Davies and True (2017).

Aloisea Inyumba and Women in Politics in Rwanda

From April to July 1994, the African country of Rwanda experienced mass killings of Tutsi and systematic rape of Tutsi women, sanctioned by the Hutu majority government. Around 70 per cent of the Tutsi population of Rwanda were murdered, often by Hutu civilians using machetes and clubs. The death toll was well above 500,000. The Rwandan Genocide and sexual violence ended when the Tutsi-backed Rwandan Patriotic Front (RPF) led by Paul Kagame took control of the country. Kagame served as vice president and minister of defence from 1994 to 2000. He has served as the elected president of Rwanda since 2003. Kagame is credited for restoring peace in Rwanda. But others working with him did much to set Rwanda on a pathway towards social stability and economic advancement. Aloisea Inyumba was central to those initiatives.

Aloisea Inyumba was a Tutsi born in Uganda to Rwandan parents. After completing university in Uganda, Inyumba met Paul Kagame and joined the RPF as a community organizer. For several years, she worked as the RPF's finance commissioner. In this role, she travelled extensively in Africa and beyond, covertly raising funds for the RPF's military operations. After the genocide and the creation of a new government, Inyumba was appointed as the minister of gender and social affairs. In this role, she used her organizing skills to advantage. Inyumba believed the key to peaceful reconstruction was to involve women in grass roots community development. Among other things, she encouraged women to adopt the many orphans left by the conflict, Tutsi raising Hutu and vice versa. She created a national women's movement, with groups run by local women. Under her stewardship, the Ministry of Gender and Social Affairs became a major force for good in Rwandan society and attracted programme support from international donors.

From 1999 to 2001, Inyumba served as executive secretary of the National Unity and Reconciliation Commission, where she established a programme to explain the benefits of Rwandans working together at the local level. By keeping the focus on grass roots initiatives rather than activities in the national capital, Inyumba was able to make good use of knowledge and experience recently gained in her gender and social affairs role. The peace process in Rwanda has received universal acclaim. After her work for the Reconciliation Commission, Inyumba joined Rwanda's inaugural Senate in 2004. In 2011, she returned to the government as minister for gender and family promotion, which she held until her death from cancer in late 2012.

Upon her death, tributes to Inyumba came from around the globe. One commentator noted '[h]er humility, her quiet voice and graceful manner masked a will of iron' (Melvern 2013). By 2012, Rwanda had a higher percentage of female parliamentarians than any other country in the world and women occupied more than half of the senior posts in government. Inyumba was fundamental to making that happen. Throughout her career, she promoted equality, recognizing the broad benefits of tapping the resources and talents of everyone, no matter their gender or race. Her efforts to promote strong local governance structures ensured a pipeline of talented women would flow from the grass roots to the nation's capital. For more discussion of this case, see Melvern (2013) and Munyaneza (2012).

1.3 Common Attributes of Policy Entrepreneurs

Those fitting the description of a policy entrepreneur are likely to be ambitious in pursuit of a cause, to exhibit social acuity, to be able to pass a relevant credibility test, to display sociability and to be tenacious. In their distinctive ways, the four profiled policy entrepreneurs embodied all of these attributes in pursuit of their particular policy goals. Here, we discuss each attribute in turn.

(1) Ambition: Driving a major policy innovation takes serious commitment and energy. Those who are prepared to do this must be motivated by a bigger vision for a better future (Collins 2001; Quinn 2000). Ambition for a particular cause supplies the 'why' that explains everything else

policy entrepreneurs do. Earlier, we noted Kingdon's (1984 [2011]) argument that policy entrepreneurs are defined by their willingness to invest various resources in the hope of a future return. Ambition leads people to make such investments. Further, the energy and commitment they display in pursuit of a cause enhance their credibility. As they display ambition, policy entrepreneurs get others to believe in what they are seeking to do and to join their endeavours.

(2) Social Acuity: Policy entrepreneurship requires high levels of social acuity. Opportunities to promote policy innovations do not come along with labels on them. They need to be perceived within complex social and political contexts. Through their social acuity, policy entrepreneurs discover how people are thinking about problems. They come to appreciate the concerns and motivations that drive others. And they develop ideas about how to construct effective advocacy efforts, how to make most use of networks of contacts and what kinds of political support, policy arguments and evidence will serve them best in particular policymaking venues.

(3) Credibility: Policy entrepreneurship involves promoting policy innovations through building strong coalitions of support. To attract others to work with them, policy entrepreneurs must be deemed highly credible. They can achieve credibility in a number of ways. These include demonstrating expertise in a particular field, holding particular positions within or around government, or having a compelling narrative of their lives and their past achievements. Others will commit to causes only where the leading figures strike them as having what it takes to make a difference.

(4) Sociability: Although they choose particular policy innovations to advocate, policy entrepreneurs must always consider how others will respond to their ideas and ambitions. Policy entrepreneurs must possess the ability to empathize with others and understand other people's needs. This calls for high levels of sociability. Sociability is both conceptually and operationally different from social acuity. For all politicians, sociability is the lifeblood. It grants them the ability to go from discerning points of common interest between themselves and others to engaging with others in ways that make those others feel appreciated. Effective policy entrepreneurs use their sociability to expand their networks and build advocacy coalitions. In the process, they often help others to see how their specific actions can contribute to the bigger vision for policy change.

(5) Tenacity: Finally, policy entrepreneurs must be tenacious (Duckworth 2016; Mintrom 1997a; Quinn and Quinn 2009). We define tenacity as the willingness to keep working towards a bigger goal, even when that goal seems nowhere in sight. This quality is important because entrepreneurs

typically operate in contexts that are highly complex and where the chances of achieving success can seem slim. Conveying the significance of a change effort can assist policy entrepreneurs as they seek to maintain the focus and commitment of those working with them.

Taken together, the attributes of policy entrepreneurs reviewed here offer important insights into how they tend to manifest themselves in the world, and how they work with others. Looking back to the four profiles of policy entre-preneurs, we can see that each of them displayed these attributes in their distinctive ways. There is no question that they were each ambitious for major causes. In their various ways, they each advocated policy innovations that had profound effects. Significantly, those effects were dynamic. That is to say, the changes they introduced motivated others to initiate additional changes. This is seen clearly in the case of Ken Livingstone and his efforts to have cities engage in coordinated action to both reduce and adapt to climate change. All four of them found ways to demonstrate their credibility in promoting policy change. Sometimes they drew upon their past experiences. Aloisea Inyumba did that, parlaying her community-organizing credentials to promote reconciliation in Rwanda and help put the country on a path to peace and prosperity. The featured policy entrepreneurs also exhibited social acuity and sociability, especially in the ways that they pulled together advocacy coalitions in support of their policy goals. Finally, they were tenacious. In all cases they were promoting policy changes that were audacious in scope and that were susceptible to being hindered or undermined by those not sharing their enthusiasms.

1.4 Defining Terms

Earlier, I suggested that we should avoid a situation where all forms of political action are viewed as variations upon policy entrepreneurship. We should also be concerned that all forms of policy change may be labelled as policy innovations. To assist here, I briefly define terms as they will appear throughout this Element. As the four aforementioned examples of policy entrepreneurs illustrate, policy entrepreneurs take actions that disrupt the status quo. Policy entrepreneurs introduce new ideas for public policy into relevant policymaking domains or contexts. Long ago, Everett Rogers (1962 [2003]) provided a definitive descrip-tion of an innovation as follows: '[a]n *innovation* is an idea, practice, or object that is perceived as new by an individual or other unit of adoption. It matters little, so far as human behaviour is concerned, whether or not an idea is objectively new as measured by the lapse of time since its first use or discovery' (p. 11). Extending from here, we might say that policy innovation involves the introduction of a new idea and its design and implementation in a particular context. A policy idea considered part of the status quo in one jurisdiction may be considered a policy innovation in another jurisdiction, if that other jurisdiction is yet to adopt it. Questions about the significance of a specific policy innovation cannot be easily answered without reference to the jurisdictional context. It is quite plausible that a policy innovation considered trivial at a national level might loom as highly significant at a local level.

Policy entrepreneurs must use their capabilities to promote their new ideas in given jurisdictions. How policy entrepreneurs activate their capabilities to manoeuvre through the constraints of a given jurisdictional context and its political institutions in ways that both protect and promote their new ideas will demonstrate their entrepreneurial skill. A policy entrepreneur able to present a new idea as consistent with the status quo, or as a minor modification of it, will face less resistance and will require less capability than one who explicitly seeks to promote a radical departure from current policies and practices. So the nature of the policy idea is central to understanding what capabilities policy entrepreneurs need and how those capabilities can be utilized in the specific jurisdictional context in which they seek to secure policy innovation.

Often in this text, I explore how policy entrepreneurs can catalyse dynamic change. As discussed later, dynamic change occurs when a change in one jurisdiction serves to promote similar change in other jurisdictions. Sometimes, these processes of dynamic change are termed policy innovation diffusion. The claim made throughout this Element is that policy entrepreneurs are vital actors in driving this kind of change.

1.5 Studying Policy Entrepreneurs

Interest in policy entrepreneurs has increased considerably since this way of describing key policy actors was first coined. This section introduced what policy entrepreneurs do and attributes they often possess. Section 2 reviews what we know regarding common political strategies that policy entrepreneurs deploy in pursuit of their policy goals. Section 3 explores how the concept of the policy entrepreneur intersects with traditional theories of the policymaking process. It clarifies how policy entrepreneurs 'fit in' and why they are important actors to study. Section 4 seeks to dispel any notion that policy entrepreneurs experience success or failure purely as a result of their own actions. This section reviews how policy entrepreneurs interact with their contexts and considers how the presence or absence of a few common contextual factors can greatly influence the likelihood of success or failure for would-be agents of policy change. Section 5 suggest directions for future research on policy entrepreneurs and their promotion of dynamic change. It suggests several highly promising paths forwards for study of these actors and their impact on public policy. Section 6, the concluding section, comes back to the claim that policy entrepreneurs represent an extremely interesting and important class of political actors. Here, the argument is made that policy entrepreneurship will likely become even more essential in the coming decades as social, technological and environmental changes drive demand for a range of shifts in public policy settings at all levels of government.

2 What Policy Entrepreneurs Do

Policy entrepreneurs reveal themselves through their attempts to transform policy ideas into policy innovations and, hence, disrupt status quo policy arrangements. This distinguishes them from many interest group leaders, for whom maintenance of current institutional settings and power relations is paramount. In studying the political work of policy entrepreneurs, we can gain insights into what it takes to promote significant policy change. To begin such a study, we need a means of identifying policy entrepreneurs. A good place to start is by looking for people who are seeking to introduce new policy ideas and, in the process, drive significant policy change. Those efforts might involve introducing wholly new policies within specific jurisdictions. They might involve building upon particular policies that are already in place. We can expect to find great diversity in the policy issues that policy entrepreneurs care about and their reasons for caring about them. However, given their common goal of promoting significant policy change, we might expect their actions to follow certain patterns.

What does policy entrepreneurship involve? In recent years, political scientists have started to systematically study the actions of policy entrepreneurs. These studies have considered the actions of individuals and those working with them across many different policymaking contexts, from the local to the global. This section reviews the state of knowledge on common actions of policy entrepreneurs. It builds from earlier investigations by Kingdon (1984 [2011]), Mintrom (2000) and Roberts and King (1996). For some years now, we have understood that policy entrepreneurs work at problem framing, team building and networking. In recent years, additions to the literature have placed the spotlight on other actions, including leading by example and exploring ways to scale-up change processes (Frisch-Aviram, Cohen and Beeri 2019; Mintrom and Luetjens 2017; Mintrom and Thomas 2018). Growing awareness of common regularities in the actions of policy entrepreneurs also serves to underscore an even more fundamental action. That is, thinking strategically.

In reviewing common actions of policy entrepreneurs, I do not seek to rank the relative importance of each. My starting point is the expectation that all policy entrepreneurs perform these actions to a greater or lesser extent. Some will rely more heavily on specific actions rather than others. This will reflect the nature of the political context they are operating in and their own capabilities. For example, some policy entrepreneurs might show themselves to be highly adept at framing or reframing policy problems. In the process, they can make it easier to draw together coalitions of people supporting the policy changes they are promoting. At other times, policy entrepreneurs might display considerable strength in networking. Those who are adept at networking across jurisdictions can often identify policy ideas and advocacy strategies that they can subsequently utilize in their own jurisdictions. However, to do this well, they must either have sound networks in and around local policymaking venues, or be highly effective at working with people who do. As we will see, all of the actions reviewed in this section indicate a need for well-honed social skills. That is why social acuity and sociability are included among the key attributes of policy entrepreneurs introduced in Section 1.

2.1 Thinking Strategically

When people think strategically, they choose a particular goal and then determine the set of actions they will need to take and the resources they will require to pursue that goal. Strategy is made challenging by the presence of other people and the uncertainty and potential turbulence others create for you as they choose their own goals and likewise figure out ways to achieve them. We should never assume that other people's observed actions and behaviours will remain unchanged in the face of our own interventions. In the language of game theory, strategic thinking is necessary in many situations because we are acting in conditions that are subject to continual change through the behaviour of other rational actors (Dixit and Nalebuff 2008). In our professional lives, all of us face incentives to think and act strategically. Indeed, postgraduate training in areas like public management and business typically place great emphasis on imparting strategic thinking skills. Yet, even in the absence of formal training, many people still figure out effective strategies for achieving their goals (Mazzeo, Oyer and Schaefer 2014).

Given their desire to promote policy innovations, policy entrepreneurs must be highly strategic actors. Kingdon (1984 [2011]) famously observed that policy entrepreneurs take advantage of 'windows of opportunity' in the policy-making process. This is where an alignment appears to exist between prevailing political conditions, the problem the policy entrepreneur seeks to address and the appetite for applying the policy entrepreneur's preferred policy solution. Of course, such windows of opportunity must be perceived. Political actors need to have extremely good interpretative skills to be able to sense these moments within the broader buzz and confusion that often emanates from the world of politics and policymaking. This is what makes strategic thinking all the more vital and, at the same time, all the more challenging for people seeking to drive policy change.

Beyond the 'high strategy' requirements of policy entrepreneurship, there are many other kinds of strategic action that policy entrepreneur, and policy professionals, in general, can take to raise their performance and the likelihood that they will attain their policy goals. In this regard, Thomas Kalil (2017) provided several useful insights based on his tours of duty as a senior advisor – and self-styled policy entrepreneur – in the White House during the Clinton and Obama administrations. Among other things, Kalil emphasized the importance of starting out with a clear goal in mind, having a large and growing 'toolbox' of policy solutions that could be applied to address specific problems, and developing effective ways to work with others and reduce the barriers to others supporting your proposals. Of course, these actions are not the exclusive domain of policy entrepreneurs. Just like a range of people skills (Mintrom 2003), they are as essential to being a high-performing policy professional as they are to engaging in policy entrepreneurship. In operating environments where everyone faces strong incentives to be highly professional and highly strategic, policy entrepreneurs must be adept at playing the game. In the absence of adequate experience as policy professionals, or excellent working relationships with others that can compensate for behavioural or strategic deficits, would-be policy entrepreneurs will be non-starters in driving policy change.

2.2 Framing Problems

The political dynamics of problem definition have been explored extensively by policy scholars over the past few decades (Allison 1971; Baumgartner and Jones 1993; Nelson 1984; Rochefort and Cobb 1994; Schneider and Ingram 1993; Schön and Rein 1994). Problems in the policy realm invariably come with multiple attributes. How those problems get framed – or what attributes are made salient in policy discussions – can determine which individuals and groups will pay attention to them. This suggests that advocates of policy change can improve their chances of building winning coalitions if they portray problems in new ways (see, e.g., Stone 1997). Problem framing, then, can be used to shape how people relate specific problems to their own interests. Viewed in this way, framing of policy problems is always a political act. Effective problem framing requires the combination of social acuity with skills in conflict management and negotiation (Fisher, Ury and Patton 1991; Heifetz 1994).

There are several common tactics that policy entrepreneurs use when framing problems. Among other things, these tactics include presenting evidence in ways that suggest a crisis is at hand (Nelson 1984; Stone 1997), finding ways to highlight failures of current policy settings (Baumgartner and Jones 1993; Henig 2008) and drawing support from actors beyond the immediate scope of the problem (Levin and Sanger 1994; Roberts and King 1991; Schattschneider 1960). Recent work by Dewulf and Bouwen (2012) has emphasized the interactional nature of problem framing. This casts policy entrepreneurs as conversationalists who construct the meaning of situations through discussion with others, rather than as architects who establish frames in advance of discussion, with the intention of using rhetorical skills to persuade others to adopt them as is.

Section 1 contained a profile of Ken Livingstone, former mayor of London. Livingstone's actions led to the creation of the highly influential C40 group. His actions offer a lesson in the power of problem framing. Livingstone's fundamental problem framing act involved representing cities – rather than nation-states – as central agents in the response to climate change. This framing was significant. By framing climate change as a fundamental issue facing urban populations, Livingstone showed other city leaders how to assert themselves as key players on climate change policy (Betsill and Bulkeley 2007). Members of the group subsequently came to frame the increasing pressures that cities are facing – population growth, planning policy, infrastructure provision and so on – as presenting major opportunities to lower their carbon footprint through more efficient infrastructure and planning (Kern and Bulkeley 2009; Rabe 2004; Victor, House and Joy 2005). Further, Livingstone's framing of climate change as an urgent matter also helped him advance the view that there are already many helpful practical actions being taken in cities around the world. As Livingstone told the story, a great deal of good could be achieved – and achieved quickly – through cross-jurisdictional sharing of knowledge of what works. Essentially, Livingstone was making a powerful case for cities to be viewed as key hubs for implementation of population, business and environmental policies. By promoting this portrait of cities, Livingston argued for more extensive interconnection of an already established capacity for both mitigating and adapting to climate change.

2.3 Building Teams

Like their counterparts in business, policy entrepreneurs must be team players. Individuals are often the instigators of change, but their strength does not come from the force of their ideas alone, or from their possession of superhuman powers. As Petridou (2014) has observed, 'entrepreneurial actions are carried out by teams and not just one heroic, lonely individual' (p. S22). Policy entrepreneurs gain their real strength through working effectively with others. The team-building activities of policy entrepreneurs can take several forms. First, policy entrepreneurs often work in tight-knit teams composed of individuals with different knowledge and skills, who are able to offer mutual support in the pursuit of change (Meier 2002; Mintrom, Salisbury and Luetjens 2014; Oborn, Barrett and Exworthy 2011). Second, policy entrepreneurs make use of their personal and professional networks (Mintrom and Vergari 1998). Finally, policy entrepreneurs recognize the importance of creating and guiding advocacy coalitions to promote policy change (Mintrom 2013; Mintrom and Vergari 1996).

Policy entrepreneurs who get along well with others and who are well connected in their local policy contexts are more likely to achieve their policy goals. (Kingdon 1984 [2011]; Rabe 2004). That is because they understand the ideas, motives and concerns of the people whose support they must garner. Often, the gathering of political intelligence and development of strategy happens in team settings. A classic example was reported by Roberts and King (1996). In their study of policy entrepreneurs promoting school choice in Minnesota, these researchers observed the formation of a tight-knit team of policy entrepreneurs. The team included people outside of the legislative process who had developed ideas inspired by their grass-roots connections as well as seasoned legislators who knew every detail of parliamentary procedures and understood effective ways to secure policy change. Mintrom (2000) reported similar kinds of team interaction in other jurisdictions in the United States where school choice has been pursued.

Given their importance to supporting policy innovation, further, separate consideration will now be given to the two aforementioned variants of team building – using networks and working with advocacy coalitions.

2.4 Using and Expanding Networks

Stretching back to Mohr's (1969) study of organizational innovation and Walker's (1969) study of the spread of policy innovations, we find that those actors most able to promote change in specific contexts have typically acquired relevant knowledge from elsewhere. Kammerer and Namhata (2018) and True and Mintrom (2001), among others, have demonstrated that engagement in relevant policy networks spanning across jurisdictions can significantly increase the likelihood that advocates for policy change will achieve success.

Policy entrepreneurs understand that their networks of contacts represent repositories of skills and knowledge which they can draw upon to support their initiatives (Burt 2000; Knoke 1990). The notion of building teams of insiders and outsiders, as already noted, is relevant when we consider how policy entrepreneurs use their networks. Mintrom and Vergari (1998) showed that engagement in cross-jurisdictional networks helps policy entrepreneurs as they seek to gain legislative consideration for policy innovations. Meanwhile, for the same set of policy entrepreneurs, engagement in networks in and around government in their home jurisdictions is vital for gaining legislative adoption of those policy innovations. In short, the external ties matter for idea generation, and the diffusion of ideas. The internal ties matter for actually making change happen. These observations are consistent with the findings of Sarah Anderson, Rob DeLeo and Kristin Taylor (2019) regarding the crucial use that policy entrepreneurs make of credible information provision as they seek to gain trust with legislators and influence agenda setting.

Here, the case of William Hague and the Preventing Sexual Violence Initiative is instructive (Davies and True 2017). During his time as British foreign secretary (2010–14), Hague was most interested in driving policy changes in other countries – making sure that atrocities like those that occurred in Bosnia–Herzegovina and Rwanda in the 1990s would not happen elsewhere in the future. Towards this end, he first made sure that policy settings in the United Kingdom strongly supported his broader advocacy goals. His position of power within the UK government mattered greatly. However, he had to engage in quite different strategies outside of the United Kingdom in order to realise this particular foreign policy ambition. Hague showed himself to be masterful at using cross-jurisdictional networks to support his policy goal. Specifically, he saw the G8 Summit of 2013 as a key moment for influence on other powerful governments. From his point of centrality, given Britain's presidency of the G8 at that time, Hague worked to achieve agreement across G8 members to a statement of commitment to ending sexual violence in conflict. In the process, he thought carefully about the kinds of information he needed to amass and the actions he needed to take to draw attention to the issue and have other governments recognize it as a matter of fundamental importance. He used and expanded his external networks in pursuit of the Preventing Sexual Violence Initiative.

2.5 Working with Advocacy Coalitions

Working with advocacy coalitions is closely related to building teams and making use of network connections. Paul Sabatier (1988) developed the

Advocacy Coalition Framework, which has been highly influential among scholars of public policy. Sabatier (1988) defined an advocacy coalition as 'people from a variety of positions (elected and agency officials, interest group leaders, researchers, etc.) who share a particular belief system – for example, a set of basic values, causal assumptions, and problem perceptions – and who show a nontrivial degree of coordinated activity over time' (p. 139). The 'glue' that holds an advocacy coalition together is its members' shared beliefs over core policy matters. The Advocacy Coalition Framework assumes that members of coalitions will disagree often on minor matters, but that disagreement will be limited. The framework rejects the possibility that 'coalitions of convenience' motivated by 'short-term self-interest' can have lasting impacts on policy directions. Mintrom and Vergari (1996) used evidence from Michigan to show how policy entrepreneurs promoting educational change worked with and influenced an established advocacy coalition to promote policy change. While there may be times when policy entrepreneurs work to establish advocacy coalitions, it is reasonable to expect that they more frequently engage in actions that serve to build on the strengths of coalitions that already exist in some form.

The case of Bob Klein and his attempts to secure government funding for stem cell research in California offers a good example of how a policy entrepreneur can work with an advocacy coalition (Mintrom 2015). While Klein needed ultimately to convince the voters of California to support Proposition 71, he first had to engage in a great deal of intermediate work to gain support from powerful allies. He did not build a new advocacy coalition from the ground up. Rather, he found ways to bring together a range of entities already working in advocacy coalitions. Part of his genius involved encouraging these coalitions to work together in a coordinated fashion to support the policy change he was seeking. On this score, it is useful to observe that universities in the state, which stood to gain greatly from the initiative, assisted in development of the proposition. Universities have good reason to be completely across all relevant state legislation. Consequently, they could support him without deviating greatly from their standard operating procedures. Yet, in the process, they solved a potentially huge problem for Klein – how to devise a proposition that would achieve what was intended while still garnering a winning proportion of voter support. Other entities contributed in other ways, and in so doing became part of the coalition supporting the proposition.

The size of a coalition can be crucial for demonstrating the degree of support a proposal for policy change enjoys. Just as importantly, the composition of a coalition can convey the breadth of support for a proposal. That is why policy entrepreneurs often work to gain support from groups that might appear as unlikely allies for a cause. Used effectively, the composition of a coalition can help to deflect the arguments of opponents of change (Baumgartner and Jones 1993). In the case of Bob Klein with Proposition 71, he found ways to make his proposal attractive to many ordinary citizens in the state. Most obviously, he took his own story of having a son fighting debilitating diabetes to build support from others who could identify with him, or who knew of families with loved ones who could benefit from advances in stem cell research.

2.6 Leading by Example

Leadership by example is another way that policy entrepreneurs can establish credibility for themselves and their proposals for policy innovation. Leading by example is a way to make the pursuit of policy change believable. Risk aversion among decision makers presents a major challenge for actors seeking to promote significant policy change. Policy entrepreneurs often take actions intended to reduce the perception of risk among decision makers. A common strategy involves engaging with others to clearly demonstrate the workability of a policy proposal. For several decades, those promoting deregulation of infrastructural industries in the United States – both at the state and national level – relaxed regulatory oversight in advance of seeking legislative change (Derthick and Quirk 1985; Teske 2004). These pre-emptive actions reduced the ability of opponents to block change by engendering fears about possible consequences. For similar reasons, foundations have funded pilot projects associated with expansion of health insurance coverage (Oliver and Paul-Shaheen 1997), the use of school vouchers (Mintrom and Vergari 2009; Moe 1995) and support for early childhood education programmes (Knott and McCarthy 2007). In all instances, the creation of working models of the proposed change served to generate crucial information about programme effectiveness and practicality.

When they lead by example – taking an idea and turning it into action themselves – agents of change signal their genuine commitment to improved social outcomes. This can do a lot to win credibility with others, and, hence, build momentum for change (Kotter 1996; Quinn 2000). Further, when policy entrepreneurs take action, they can sometimes create situations where legislators look out of touch (Mintrom 1997a). In such situations, the risk calculations of legislators can switch from a focus on the consequences of action to a focus on the consequences of inaction.

2.7 Scaling-up Advocacy Efforts and Supporting Policy Change

Those seeking to promote broad policy change must pay careful attention to scaling-up their advocacy efforts. Often, this requires starting off by securing desired changes in one jurisdiction and then using the those changes as evidence to support changes in other jurisdictions. Earlier, we used the case of Ken Livingstone with climate change as an illustration of effective problem framing. The case also illustrates how scaling-up can occur. Livingstone was incredibly successful in building upon long-established linkages among large cities around the world to promote his agenda for action on climate change. His activism to bring other cities on board and to then create partnerships between C40 and other advocate organizations resulted in remarkable success in terms of the scaling-up of advocacy.

In a different way, William Hague was also highly successful in scaling-up support for UN Security Council Resolution 1963 and the Preventing Sexual Violence Initiative. His well-chosen actions had cascade effects that prompted further change actions led by others elsewhere around the globe. We can also see evidence of scaling-up in the attempts of Aloisea Inyumba to promote women's representation in national politics in Rwanda. While the genocide in that country resulted in a national population that comprised of a majority of women, that in itself was not sufficient to lead to the growth of women serving in major leadership roles, especially at the national level. What appears to have made a huge difference is the ways that Inyumba worked at the community level to build the pipeline of women who were interested in political office and were developing the capabilities to move from holding office at the local level to holding office at higher levels, including the national level. As with Livingstone and Hague, Inyumba's actions were carefully devised, and first involved creating good practices that built solid foundations that subsequently supported scaling-up.

2.8 Conclusion

This Element opened with a discussion of why policy entrepreneurs matter. This was followed by four brief profiles of specific policy entrepreneurs and the policy changes they promoted. That led to a discussion of five key attributes of policy entrepreneurs: ambition, social acuity, credibility, sociability and tenacity. In this section, we have reviewed common political strategies that policy entrepreneurs deploy in pursuit of their policy goals. Here, drawing upon evidence from a broad set of studies, seven common actions of policy entrepreneurs have been discussed. They are: thinking strategically, framing problems, building teams, using and expanding networks, working with advocacy coalitions, leading by example and scaling-up advocacy efforts. Together, these common actions tell us a lot about how policy entrepreneurs work to secure significant policy change. Other things being equal, policy entrepreneurs who practice these seven actions are more likely to achieve success than those who do not. It is important to note just how socially adept and driven policy entrepreneurs must be to effectively deploy these actions.

At the same time, it must be remembered that these common actions by no means exhaust the range of activities policy entrepreneurs perform. Indeed, given that they are highly motivated and highly creative individuals, we should expect policy entrepreneurs to be continually refining their actions and figuring out new approaches to advocating for policy change. Often they do this in team-like situations, and they adjust their actions based on their assessments of the motivations and strategies of others.

Drawing policy entrepreneurs out of their political contexts, as we have done so far, can raise our awareness of who might belong to this distinct class of political actors and what we might expect to see them do. Yet there is also a risk in this approach. That is, we could easily conclude from the discussion so far that policy entrepreneurs are people who could potentially drive significant policy change no matter where they are located. In reality, policy entrepreneurs are very much shaped by their operating contexts. Section 3, our next section, offers a first step towards fully acknowledging that point and exploring its implications. The section explores how the concept of the policy entrepreneur intersects with traditional theories of the policymaking process. Section 4 continues the theme of studying policy entrepreneurs in context. It does so by considering how other factors that impact on political decision-making can influence the degree of success or failure that policy entrepreneurs meet as they seek to secure significant policy change.

3 Policy Entrepreneurs in the Policymaking Process

Policy entrepreneurs act to promote policy innovations intended to produce significant policy change. To do so, they must be immersed in policymaking processes, which are inherently political, complex and combative. Over the past half century, various theories of policymaking have been advanced and developed. This section provides a review of six major ones: incrementalism, elite theory, institutionalism, the multiple streams approach, punctuated equilibrium theory and the Advocacy Coalition Framework. In each case, after explaining key features of the theory, consideration is given to the compatibility between that theory and the concept of the policy entrepreneur. Here, then, the recurrent question is: Where do policy entrepreneurs fit in? Taking time to think about policy entrepreneurs in the policymaking process promises two pay offs. First, for researchers, it helps us to consider when and how policy entrepreneurs might be most likely to meet with success, and what combination of conditions and actions could increase their chances of securing policy change (see, e.g., Anderson, DeLeo and Taylor 2019; Bakir and Jarvis 2017; Cairney and Jones 2016; Dudley 2013). Second, for those interested in contributing to policy development, policy advising and promoting policy change, this discussion indicates how accurate interpretation of specific policy contexts can assist in the development of strategies to gain influence. This practical aspect of the section augments other practical advice on how to have influence in policy-making (see, e.g., Kalil 2017; Mintrom 2003; Weible and Cairney 2018).

3.1 Theories of Policymaking and the Work of Policy Entrepreneurs

As theories of policymaking have been advanced and developed, a degree of borrowing has occurred, as theorists have worked to put forward new interpretations of policymaking while acknowledging earlier conceptual contributions. Despite their different perspectives, reviewing a set of influential theories together can deepen our understanding of the world in which policy entrepreneurs operate. Theorization of policymaking never ends – new contributions are continuously being made (see, e.g., Cairney 2013; Kirkpatrick and Stoutenborough 2018). This discussion is therefore necessarily limited because it does not take account of all the ways people conceptualize policymaking. That said, the intent is to give a good sense of the key concerns that are addressed in theories of the policymaking process and why those concerns matter. This will prove useful as we think further about why some policy entrepreneurs meet with success while others do not.

3.2 Incrementalism

As a theory of the policymaking process, incrementalism has been highly influential. Advanced by Charles Lindblom (1959, 1979), who often referred to it as 'muddling through', incrementalism posits that most change within policymaking occurs through small steps pursued by risk-averse policymakers. The theory owes considerable debt to Herbert Simon's (1947) notion of 'bounded rationality' and the view that decision makers tend to make satisfactory or 'satisficing' choices that are clearly within reach, rather than pursue changes that could, theoretically, yield 'maximal' benefits relative to costs. Lindblom rejected the notion that policymakers follow a rational choice strategy, in the sense of defining the problem, laying out alternative solutions, predicting the consequences, valuing the outcomes and making a choice. Even if a single actor were required to make policy in response to a given problem, complexity would soon make the exercise of rational choice impossible. The potential for rational choice in policymaking is further stymied because reasonable people can be expected to disagree about many aspects of a policy issue. Both complexity and disagreement greatly reduce the odds that bold policy responses will ever be adopted with unanimity. Incrementalism is the result.

Even though making policy change in small steps may seem frustrating, Lindblom (1968) characterized it as a 'shrewd, resourceful' way of wrestling with complex problems. In his conception of the policymaking process, he argued that focus should be placed on the behaviour of proximate policymakers. These include legislators, political executives, appointed bureaucrats and some party officials; that is, anyone with some decision-making authority. Proximate policymakers operate within a 'play of power' governed by institutional structures, or the rules of the game, that include the provisions of relevant constitutions, legislative acts, administrative rulings, executive orders and judicial decisions. Policy choices constitute products of the structured interactions among proximate policymakers. But no deterministic linkages exist between the preferences and actions of any given participants and specific policy choices.

The nature of democratic government and the separation of powers together force participants in the policymaking process to cooperate in order to achieve policy change. Lindblom characterized formal procedures, like committee decision making in legislatures, as 'islands of formal organization in a sea of informal mutual adjustment' (1968, p. 93). Often, participants consider their policy proposals from the perspective of those they seek to persuade, and they make adjustments to ensure that their proposals are attractive to others. Mutual adjustments are the means through which cooperation occurs, and policymakers are always interacting with each other in the hope of enhancing the odds that their particular policy preferences will prevail. This process of mutual adjustment often results in new policies that do not reflect anyone's original views. When persuasion does not alter the views of others, coercion can sometimes do the job – but this requires one party to have authority over another. Since not all can work power to their advantage, informal opportunities for seeking cooperation among policymakers are always more numerous than those based on coercion.

In this conception of policymaking, there is room to consider the role of the policy entrepreneur. Policy entrepreneurs might come from the ranks of proximate policymakers or they might be more on the margins of policymaking circles. According to Lindblom, the key to successfully engaging proximate policymakers is to present your argument in an appealing form. Likewise, proximate policymakers can be influenced by their assessments of the interests represented in a policy entrepreneur's coalition, and the size and strength of it.

When seeking to have influence from outside the centres of policymaking, policy entrepreneurs must be careful to cultivate close contacts with those in decision-making positions. In this way, they can demonstrate their trustworthiness and their commitment to their ideas for policy change. Provost (2003) has explored the systematic ways that state attorney generals have sought to influence policymaking in their jurisdictions. Rabe (2004) has shown how state-level policy analysts and others in bureaucratic positions can have influence when technical issues are at stake.

Incrementalism presents a frustrating inhibitor to dramatic change. However, patient actors who hold a clear vision of the end they are seeking can still move policy in directions they desire. The key is to see how a series of small changes could, over time, produce similar results as more dramatic, immediate change. To maintain a functioning coalition, under incrementalism, policy entrepreneurs must keep track of their small victories and explain to their supporters how those incremental steps are taking them in the right direction.

3.3 Elite Theory

Political scientists have often disagreed on the sources of influence on policymaking. There are several areas of contention. It is frequently said that interest groups have a lot of influence on policy choices (Baumgartner and Leech 1998). In this view, the most powerful interest groups – judged especially in terms of financial strength – are likely to have the most influence on the policy choices of elected decision makers. However, raw power is not sufficient to drive change. Those interest groups with major resources must use them in ways that shape popular ideas (Berry and Wilcox 2018). A common view is that the most influential interest groups make persuasive policy arguments and back them up with careful financial support of political candidates during elections.

Elite theory represents an important variant of interest group theories. The sociologist C. Wright Mills (1956) drew attention to the role of elites in shaping society, but his analysis left plenty of room for other social scientists to further investigate how elites maintain and reproduce themselves and their interests. Among political scientists, elite theory is most closely associated with Thomas R. Dye (1976, 2014). Dye claimed that democracy, particularly as practiced in the United States, has long been dominated by powerful elites. The theory divides society into the powerful few and the powerless, apathetic masses. Under this theory, those who are elected to legislatures or as political executives tend to come from, or be strongly supported by, the wealthiest groups in society. There is room within elite theory for individuals from non-elite backgrounds to get ahead and have influence. However, to do so, such people must generally show strong support for the values of the elites. This ability for non-elites to join the elites is considered essential to the stability of society and the avoidance of civil unrest.

Elite theory holds several important implications for how we interpret the making of public policy. First, specific areas of public policy are likely to be dominated by specific elites, reflecting their interests. For example, agricultural policy is likely to heavily reflect the interests of farmers, large agribusinesses and related industries. Likewise, healthcare policy is likely to be influenced by the interests of medical specialists, medical-equipment suppliers and pharmaceutical companies, to name some of the key players. Second, elite theory is consistent with the view that policies change slowly. Elites have established the system to work for them. They will support changes only when they are helpful for maintaining the system that confers them their power and influence. Third, elite theory suggests that the masses pay little attention to public policymaking and that they have little influence in it. Finally, elite theory posits that the ruling elites hold a broad consensus in their views on how society and politics should operate. This view again supports limited change over time, with that change happening only when it clearly aligns with the interests of elites.

Elite theory serves primarily as an explanation of the status quo in politics. To this extent, the theory offers little space for policy entrepreneurship. For change to be considered by elites, it must be seen as in their interests and as being led by them. Under these conditions, policy entrepreneurs can be expected to gain most attention when they exhibit their credentials for membership of the elite. This suggests the importance of being seen as legitimate within key networks, and to be good at working closely with others who might have more insider credibility. Further, problem framing becomes fundamental. Through initiatives to frame and reframe specific policy problems, it might be possible for policy entrepreneurs to win support for change from members of political elites. Although the conditions for securing change seem especially tough when viewed through the lens of elite theory, it is also important to remember that, historically, elites have changed their minds on important issues. Examples include the ending of the slave trade to North America (Broich 2017; Metaxas 2007), the development of the welfare state (Klein 2006) and many initiatives to expand access to schooling and university (Mettler 2007; Tyack 1974).

3.4 Institutionalism

Through much of the twentieth century, institutional accounts of government processes tended to be highly descriptive in nature, setting forth the broad features of government agencies and areas of government activity, and making normative assumptions about how people acted within them. As Herbert Simon (1947) noted, this resulted in little consideration being given to the actual behaviour of individuals within those institutions. For this reason, when political scientists became enamoured with behaviourism and how individuals respond to outside incentives and constraints, institutionalism went out of fashion as a way of interpreting policymaking processes (Easton 1969). This began to change when scholars like the economic historian Douglas North (1981, 1990), the sociologist Theda Skocpol and her colleagues (e.g., Evans, Rueschemeyer and Skocpol 1985) and the political scientists James March and Johan Olsen (1983, 1989) began exploring the interactions between individuals and broader institutional structures.

A range of institutionalist perspectives then emerged, all emphasizing the agency of individuals and groups within broader structures (Hall and Taylor 1996). Several highly influential lines of scholarship developed from here – often collectively referred to as 'the new institutionalism' (March and Olsen 1983; Powell and DiMaggio 1991). Despite the distinctive ways these new literatures developed, each focused on institutional design and the incentives that specific design features created to motivate individual choices and actions. For example, Mathew McCubbins and Thomas Schwartz (1984) made a classic contribution to this literature when they explored how members of the US Congress attain oversight of the bureaucracy. In so doing, they explained the rationality of particular oversight preferences, given opportunity costs, available technology and human cognitive limits. More broadly, contributions to this perspective on politics and society all share a deep interest in the interplay between structures and the effectiveness of individuals operating within or across them. Institutionalist accounts of the policy process and policy change identify considerable leeway for the actions of motivated individuals and groups to make a difference (Mettler 1998; Sheingate 2003; Tyack and Cuban 1995). However, these accounts are also useful for explaining the limits of such activism. For example, in highlighting 'the logic of appropriateness', March and Olsen (1989) explained the importance of institutional actors having deep knowledge of relevant procedures and the local norms that serve to define acceptable behaviour. An implication of the new institutionalism is that insider sensibilities are critical to effectiveness and they must inform efforts to secure major change.

Institutionalist accounts of the policy process and policy change identify considerable space for the exercise of policy entrepreneurship (Feldman and Khademian 2002; Majone 1996; March and Olsen 1989; Scharpf 1997). However, those seeking to promote dynamic policy change must appreciate the intricacies of the political systems through which change actually happens. That understanding helps us appreciate why the attempts of 'outsiders' to make change often come to nothing. We are brought back to the importance of social acuity, as discussed in Section 1. Policy entrepreneurs must be able to understand the workings of a given context without becoming so embedded in it that they lose their critical perspective and their motivation to promote policy innovations. Evidence suggests that policy entrepreneurs can be successful in this regard when they make good use of networks (Mintrom and Vergari 1998) or when they form teams that contain both 'insiders' and 'outsiders' (Kalil 2017; Mintrom, Salisbury and Luetjens 2014; Roberts and King 1996). Recent literature has highlighted the 'boundary spanning' initiatives of policy entrepreneurs (Faling et al. 2018). Boundary spanning works best when policy entrepreneurs are able to tap knowledge of distinctive institutions and institutional processes with the purpose of building support for change initiatives.

3.5 The Multiple Streams Approach

The multiple streams approach to interpreting the policymaking process was put forward by John Kingdon (1984 [2011]). Kingdon drew inspiration for this work from an earlier conception of organizational decision-making, the famous 'garbage can' model developed by Michael Cohen, James March and Johan Olsen (1972). This etymology of Kingdon's work is crucial to know, because it grounds his model in the tradition of decision-making analysis that directly links back to Herbert Simon's (1947) work on bounded rationality and organizational behaviour. Conceptual connections exist between incrementalism, the new institutionalism and the multiple streams approach. In this approach, attention is focused on how specific policy problems and solutions attain prominence at certain times. Yet the insights derived here have much in common with insights that Lindblom developed in his model of incrementalism and the actions of proximate policymakers.

Kingdon argued that agenda setting and policy change emerge through a combination of actions by participants and the operations of formal and informal social processes. Many individuals can call increasing attention through their various actions to specific policy issues. But it is primarily elected officials who decide which issues will become agenda items and hence set the scene for discussion of new policies or policy change. Kingdon emphasized the important role that informal communication channels play in supporting the rise of policy issues to prominence. A range of individuals collectively serve to make up specialized policy communities or networks: elected officials, bureaucrats, interest group representatives, researchers and engaged citizens.

Kingdon argued that policy issues emerge on government decision-making agendas as the result of developments in three separate process streams: the problem stream, the policy stream and the political stream. He claimed that policy entrepreneurs often serve to join the three independent streams through their efforts to bring specific problems and policy innovations to prominence. In this way, they significantly raise the likelihood that specific policy issues will stimulate policy change. Kingdon's model of policymaking is central to our discussion, because, in elaborating it, Kingdon crystalized the concept of the policy entrepreneur. To this point, the notion of entrepreneurial behaviour within policymaking processes had received very limited attention.

In the multiple streams approach, the problem stream is where actions are taken to draw attention to certain issues and to encourage a public policy response. Much is at stake when it comes to problem definition. Those benefitting from the status quo face incentives to convince others that no problem worthy of government attention exists. Those seeking to highlight a problem, aside from demonstrating the problem's significance, must show that policy solutions are available. Thus, policymakers often undertake problem definition with specific policy solutions in mind. Further, solutions sometimes chase problems. Those who think they have found a clever policy solution will look for ways to 'hook' it to a specific problem.

The policy stream is the second that Kingdon highlights. In this stream, communities of policy specialists generate and debate numerous ideas for policy solutions or viable policy alternatives. Occasionally, members of these communities come up with new ideas for policy solutions, but mostly they work with old ideas, thinking about ways to reformulate them or combine them with others. Even though ideas often sweep policy communities like fads, governments typically react quite slowly in response. To survive, ideas must be perceived as workable and feasible, and must be compatible with the values of a majority of specialists in the relevant policy community.

The political stream is the third in this conception of policymaking. This stream is composed of things like election results, changes in administrations, changes in the partisan or ideological distribution of legislatures, interest-group pressure campaigns, and changes in public opinion or the national mood. Changes in the political stream and occasional changes in the problem stream, like focusing events, provide the major opportunities for agenda changes in government. Agenda change can come rapidly at times, but organized political forces can serve as a brake. And, indeed, rapid change in the policy agenda might not produce rapid change in actual policy. For even the possibility of major policy change to arise, serious amounts of bargaining and coalition building in the political stream typically must occur.

In Kingdon's telling, agenda change emerges when the three process streams are joined. At critical times, dubbed windows of opportunity, the conditions in

all three streams favour a joining of problems, solutions and political momentum. To join the three streams, policy entrepreneurs must judge that the time is
right. They 'lie in wait in and around government with their solutions at hand,
waiting for problems to float by to which they can attach their solutions, waiting
for developments in the political stream they can use to their advantage' (p.
165). Kingdon's multiple streams approach has informed the work of many
scholars of policy change. His portrait of policy entrepreneurs as agents of
change – people who make connections across disparate groups, and engage
with proximate policymakers – has also been influential. Taking Kingdon's
work as a point of departure, several efforts have been made to advance
discussion of timing in the policy process (Baumgartner and Jones 1993;
Geva-May 2004; Herweg, Zahariadis and Zohlnhöfer 2018). In other works
influenced by Kingdon, closer attention has been paid to the identification of
policy entrepreneurs and the analysis of their actions (Mintrom 2000;
Narbutaite Aflaki, Miles and Petridou 2015).

3.6 Punctuated Equilibrium Theory

A discrepancy exists between the accounts of why policy change occurs slowly
and the multiple streams approach, which opens space for instances of dramatic
policy shifts. In seeking to reconcile these different accounts, Frank R.
Baumgartner and Bryan D. Jones developed their theory of the policy process
as one characterized by punctuated equilibrium. In this conception, policymaking
in specific areas of activity, such as healthcare or environmental protection, are
often characterized by long periods of stability interrupted by moments of abrupt,
significant change (Baumgartner and Jones 1993). As in Lindblom's account,
Baumgartner and Jones suggest that stability is the product of the limited ability
for legislators to deal with more than a few issues at a time. Stability is further
supported by the development of policy monopolies, controlled by people who
go to considerable lengths to promote positive images of current policy settings
and deflect calls for change. In this interpretation of policymaking, the task for
advocates of policy change is to bring the policy issues out into the public arena
and invoke a groundswell of change-forcing interest. Even within stable systems,
the potential for change exists. The challenge for those seeking such change is to
undermine existing present policy images and create new ones that emphasize
major problems and why the status quo is not sustainable.

Under stable policy monopolies, members of the broader policy domain and
interested citizens defer to the judgement of experts who have specialized
knowledge of their specific policy area. This knowledge might include a full
understanding of the scope and limits of the relevant laws, the organization and

allocation of power within the supporting bureaucratic structures, and relevant technical issues. Deference of this sort ensures that policy monopolies are immune from interference by outsiders. But this system of deference and non-interference is largely contingent on the public's continuing to receive positive images regarding activities in the specific policy area. Negative images can serve as cues to alert politicians that policy reform may be needed. Such reform is expected to manifest itself through non-incremental policy change, and this can bring an established way of doing things to an end.

Baumgartner and Jones note that it is possible for policy changes to occur in multiple venues. When policy change appears blocked at one level (e.g., the national government level), it might be effectively pursued elsewhere (e.g., at the state or local level). The insight here is that any attempts to establish new ways of doing things open the possibility of creating momentum for change across a whole system. For example, many state-level leaders in the United States have introduced major changes that other states subsequently adopted. Further, these state-level changes can serve to change conversations at the federal level.

In this interpretation of policymaking and policy change, the task for the policy entrepreneur is to bring the policy issues out into the public domain and attempt to invoke a swell of interest intended to induce major change. Even within stable systems, the potential for change exists. For policy entrepreneurs, the challenge is to undermine the present policy images and create new ones that emphasize major problems and a need for change. Drawing upon the work of Baumgartner and Jones (1993), several studies have subsequently explored linkages between the actions of policy entrepreneurs and the initiation of dynamic policy change. These include contributions by John (1999, 2003), Peters (1994) and True (2000).

3.7 The Advocacy Coalition Framework

The Advocacy Coalition Framework owes its genesis to Paul A. Sabatier's (1988) theorization of policy change, which has been extensively developed in subsequent decades (e.g., Sabatier and Jenkins-Smith 1993; Weible and Sabatier 2009). According to Sabatier, advocacy coalitions consist of 'people from a variety of positions (e.g., elected and agency officials, interest group leaders, researchers) who share a specific belief system – i.e., a set of basic values, causal assumptions, and problem perceptions – and who show a non-trivial degree of coordinated activity over time' (Sabatier 1988, p. 139). Coalition participants seek to ensure the maintenance and evolution of policy in specific areas, such as public schooling, healthcare and environmental protection.

The Advocacy Coalition Framework tells us how ideas for change emerge from dedicated people who coalesce around an issue. Within the Advocacy Coalition Framework, change comes from both internal and external sources. But, to have political effect, those catalysts for change need to be appropriately interpreted and translated. This process of translation takes, for example, objective social, economic and environmental conditions and portrays them in ways designed to increase the likelihood that they will receive the decision makers' attention.

The value of the Advocacy Coalition Framework lies in its emphasis on policymaking involving a large number of actors and organizations. Policy change emerges out of conversations that take place among these entities. Shared meanings and new interpretations operate as mechanisms for making sense of specific new developments – which can emerge from changes in the natural environment, technical innovation or political realignments. The quality of the collective interactions in the coalition and the coordination ability of those seeking to promote policy change greatly affect the likelihood that change will occur.

The Advocacy Coalition Framework tells us how ideas for change emerge from dedicated people that coalesce around an issue. Policy entrepreneurship is not treated explicitly within the framework. However, there is considerable room for compatibility between explanations of policy change grounded in the Advocacy Coalition Framework and those grounded in a focus on policy entrepreneurship. For example, within the Advocacy Coalition Framework, change is anticipated to come from both endogenous and exogenous shocks. But, to have political effect, those shocks need to be interpreted and translated. This process of translation is directly equivalent to the process of problem definition, whereby objective social, economic and environmental conditions are portrayed in ways that increase the likelihood that they will receive the attention desired of decision makers.

Policy entrepreneurs typically display skills needed to do this kind of translational and definitional work. Mintrom and Vergari (1996) considered the link between formation and maintenance of advocacy coalitions and the activities of policy entrepreneurs. In that account, emphasis was given to how policy entrepreneurs define problems in ways that maximize opportunities for bringing on board coalition partners. The value to advocacy coalitions of strong team builders was also emphasized and demonstrated empirically. In subsequent studies, drawing on empirical evidence across a range of policy areas and policymaking venues, Goldfinch and 't Hart (2003), Hajime (1999), Litfin (2000) and Meijerink (2005), among others, have indicated the merits of incorporating a discussion of policy entrepreneurship within discussions of advocacy coalitions.

3.8 Opportunities for Policy Entrepreneurship

The consensus emerging through this review of theories of policymaking is that policy change typically occurs incrementally. A range of factors serve to maintain the status quo. These include established institutional arrangements, established and powerful interests, and the combination of information problems and risk-aversion on the part of key decision makers. Nonetheless, instances arise where problems are broadly acknowledged as important and urgent and not readily addressed within existing policy settings. The concept of policy entrepreneurship helps us make sense of what happens in and around policy communities during these times. But the value of policy entrepreneurship as a concept is greatly increased when it is integrated with broader theorizations of the sources of policy stability and policy change. Our purpose here has been to show how that can be achieved. Along the way, references have been made to empirical studies produced in the past two decades that have started to join the concept of policy entrepreneurship with other explanations of policy change.

The foregoing discussion offers some critical insights into how we might make sense of policy change and the role of policy entrepreneurs in catalysing such change. Let us assume that an instance has arisen of dynamic policy change. For example, the legislature in a specific jurisdiction might have adopted a new policy that creates incentives for businesses to significantly reduce the amount of waste that would once have been shipped to landfill sites. How might we begin to investigate the political processes that led to that legislative change? And how might we seek to identify if and how policy entrepreneurship played a fundamental role?

The theories of the policymaking process reviewed here suggest a line of investigation. First, we would need to explore the nature of the status quo in this area of public policy before the legislative change. It would be useful to understand how this jurisdiction has been approaching environmental and sustainability issues over the past decade or so. In the process of this investigation, it would be vital to identify the key institutional arrangements that contribute to the maintenance of the status quo. What systems have been in place to guide businesses when it comes to decisions over the generation and disposal of waste products? To what degree has waste disposal been regulated and what government agencies have been involved in regulatory enforcement? As we pursue this line of inquiry, inevitably we will begin to become aware of the various stakeholders in this area of public policy. Interest group theory and our appreciation for the power of elites would guide us to identify and map out the key players and the power relationships that exist among them. It would be helpful to know how past laws and institutional arrangements have served to shape those interests and their influence strategies. Further, by exploring in this way, we are likely to develop an awareness of how disposal of waste came to be construed as a significant policy issue, one that could not be effectively addressed within existing ways of doing things.

At this point, insights from incrementalism could prove useful. We could make a timeline of relevant legislative changes over recent years in this jurisdiction that relate to environmental protection and sustainability. Such work would help to reveal the key players involved in driving or resisting previous change efforts. This is how we could gain insights into the existence of relevant advocacy coalitions and the political dynamics within them. Most critically, this work would allow us to identify people who could likely inform us on the extent to which specific individuals and teams of actors displayed the common attributes of policy entrepreneurs and deployed the kinds of strategies they use.

Ultimately, we could use interviews or surveys to systematically explore the extent to which policy entrepreneurship was a factor in prompting change. Note, however, that this approach to conducting our research ensures that we explore policy entrepreneurship in context. That is, even as we might seek to identify policy entrepreneurs who were crucial to driving the new policy that created incentives for businesses to significantly reduce the amount of waste, we do so while fully acknowledging that policy entrepreneurs operate in complicated contexts where the influences of the past, of institutional arrangements and of powerful interests are ever present.

3.9 Conclusion

The argument of this Element is that policy entrepreneurs are energetic actors who engage in collaborative actions in and around government to promote policy innovations leading to significant policy change. This section has offered a review of major theories of the policymaking process. Some of those theories have explicitly acknowledged the work of policy entrepreneurs. Others have not. Yet, in their various ways, all of these theories have helped us to further appreciate the complex context in which any actors seeking to promote policy change must operate. The forces serving to maintain the status quo can be powerful. In many ways this is entirely appropriate. To make that point is not to cast a vote for conservatism. Rather, the point is made to acknowledge the huge benefits that individuals and societies reap from the durability of effective and predictable 'rules of the game' that let us all know how things work around here.

At the same time, we must acknowledge that forces for change are always around us. The challenge for any decision-making body is to appreciate those forces and to recognize when policy responses are needed and the shape that those responses should take. Effective systems need smart people willing to constantly discuss and debate the consequences –including the trade-offs – associated with both stability and change. Policy entrepreneurs can make significant contributions to policymaking processes through their willingness to drive change initiatives. In this section, we have explored the question of where policy entrepreneurs fit in to policymaking processes. Clearly, much room exists for them to instigate change, although frequently such endeavours will meet powerful resistance from a variety of sources. In the next section, we continue this discussion of policy entrepreneurs and their operating contexts. There we consider more systematically how contexts influence the choices made by policy entrepreneurs and how we might assess the impacts of their actions.

4 Interpreting Contexts and Assessing Impacts

When we talk about policy entrepreneurs, there can be a tendency to rarify them – to fixate on who they are and the actions they take without paying sufficient attention to the contexts they operate within. Our discussion in the previous section took us some way in terms of appreciating the nature of the policy-making contexts policy entrepreneurs must negotiate. In this section, we continue that discussion, doing so with reference to some key studies of policy entrepreneurship. When political scientists first began noting the presence and actions of policy entrepreneurs, the portraits presented were sketchy, surrounded with darkness. Much about why they appeared when they did and why they took specific actions remained mysterious. Mark Schneider and Paul Teske (1992), frustrated by these isolated sightings and descriptions, scattered across multiple literatures, engaged in a 'stalking' exercise. In the process, they presented a line of research intended to transform 'the notion of entrepreneurs from the study of heroic figures to the study of a larger class of individuals who help propel political and policy changes' (p. 737). The analytical rigour of their research set the stage for a flourishing of studies of policy entrepreneurs. Those studies have brought policy entrepreneurs into the light, so we can better appreciate how they drive dynamic change.

This section proceeds as follows. First, I review the work of Schneider and Teske (1992), focusing on their efforts to understand what factors appear to lead policy entrepreneurs to become active in some contexts while remaining absent in others. Second, I review Michael Mintrom's (1997b) exploration of policy entrepreneurs and their impacts on policy change. Third, I review several studies that have subsequently explored the effectiveness of specific strategies used by policy entrepreneurs. Finally, I discuss the link between the actions of individual policy entrepreneurs and the emergence of dynamic change. How might we explain the momentum often seen in change processes, where policy innovations adopted in a handful of places catch on and rapidly spread across multiple jurisdictions? Over recent decades, a number of studies have tackled that question directly. In so doing, they have advanced our understanding of dynamic change and how it arises.

4.1 Exploring the Emergence of Policy Entrepreneurs

In their systematic hunt for policy entrepreneurs, Mark Schneider and Paul Teske (1992) began by considering what conditions might create opportunities within specific jurisdictions that would prompt a potential entrepreneur to become active. They also considered what features of the 'organizational milieu' in those jurisdictions would throw up problems that policy entrepreneurs would seek to address. In taking this approach, Schneider and Teske sought to isolate plausible motives for individuals to solve problems of collective action – that is, problems at the heart of political life. With the ambition of establishing an empirical foundation to support rigourous theory testing, the authors focused their attention on suburban communities in the United States. Thousands of such communities exist. Schneider and Teske began their sample construction with all incorporated suburbs with populations greater than 2,500 located in the 100 largest metropolitan regions of the United States. This produced a set of over 1,400 suburbs in fifty-five metropolitan regions, from which municipal clerks in 963 communities responded to their survey questions concerning the presence and activities of policy entrepreneurs. The researchers combined this survey-based evidence with census data, capturing a variety of characteristics of each community in the study.

In 257 of the 963 responses they obtained, Schneider and Teske were advised of the presence and actions of policy entrepreneurs. This suggested that around 27 per cent of communities in the study had witnessed acts of policy entrepreneurship. While Schneider and Teske were very interested in the substance of those political actions – and went on to produce a range of studies exploring them – in their initial analysis, they focused on the presence or absence of policy entrepreneurs and what might account for sightings in some places and not in others.

Schneider and Teske (1992) discovered that specific local conditions seemed to drive the emergence of local policy entrepreneurs. In particular, while controlling for a plausible set of government revenue, government spending and demographic variables, they found that entrepreneurs were more likely to be present in communities characterized by relatively high proportions of home ownership, population growth, racial diversity and property taxes. In addition, entrepreneurs were more commonly found in communities where there was significant potential for discretionary spending of local government money. Schneider and Teske interpreted these results to support their theory that entrepreneurial actors respond to incentives. If local government finances create opportunities for taking policy action, then entrepreneurs are more likely to emerge. Further, the entrepreneurial actors need to be aware of collective action problems worth addressing. Schneider and Teske contended that such problems would be more apparent in communities with citizens who had strong stakes in continuously improving material conditions, and where a degree of dynamism was present that could create political debate. High taxes, population growth and diversity all contribute to that kind of dynamism. In related research, the authors explored how, among other things, entrepreneurship could be seen in pro-growth and anti-growth movements, and how the actions of highly motivated businesses and individuals could promote political change (see Schneider and Teske, with Mintrom, 1995).

Subsequent scholarship has built on and further developed Schneider and Teske's approach to investigating policy entrepreneurship (see, e.g., Brouwer 2015; Mack, Green and Vedlitz 2008). Notably, Scott Kalafatis and Maria Carmen Lemos (2017) adapted Schneider and Teske's methods to explore the emergence of climate change policy entrepreneurs. In that study, the focus was on responses to survey questions provided by municipal clerks in 371 mid-sized cities spread across the Great Lakes region of the United States. Applying a variation on validation methods developed by Schneider and Teske (1992), the authors used a follow-up survey to confirm the presence of policy entrepreneurs and further investigate their actions. This research design allowed for identification of multiple policies entrepreneurs in the same city, appreciating that, simultaneously, different policy entrepreneurs might be promoting economic development, sustainability and policies to address climate change. Kalafatis and Lemos found that climate change policy entrepreneurs were more likely to emerge in cities where there was a relatively high degree of political fragmentation – that is to say, small cities located in regions with many similarly small cities surrounding them, and where council members directly represented districts, rather than being chosen by the winning party. They also found climate change policy entrepreneurs were more likely to emerge in cities where other policy entrepreneurs were advocating policies to promote environmental sustainability.

The nature of Kalafatis and Lemos's (2017) research design allowed them to speculate further on how jurisdictional fragmentation might support policy diffusion. Successful policy entrepreneurship can be seen and possibly emulated by more individuals in the more fragmented system. Through this process, the authors contend that 'consciously or unconsciously', the first climate change policy entrepreneur in such an urban region could initiate 'a significant disruption in ongoing regional policy activity' (p. 1796). We see here how a focus on the factors promoting the emergence of policy entrepreneurs can also begin to explain their impact on broader, dynamic policy change. We return to this matter later in the section.

4.2 Exploring the Impact of Policy Entrepreneurs

Until Mark Schneider and Paul Teske launched their project to systematically identify entrepreneurial actors in local government settings, all examinations of policy entrepreneurship had been case study-based. Such work has great value, and it continues to contribute to our understandings of policy entrepreneurship. At the same time, case studies of policy entrepreneurs are vulnerable to the risk of missing vital aspects of the broader context that can help to explain observed instances of political success or failure. Inspired by Schneider and Teske's project, Michael Mintrom (1997b) produced a study of policy entrepreneurs operating at the state government level across the United States. In this work, Mintrom sought to systematically study what policy entrepreneurs do and the impact of their actions on policy change, while extensively accounting for other plausible explanations of policy change. The study has been highly influential. Here, I review the key elements of the research design and findings.

Mintrom placed his focus on the trend across states in the United States in the late 1980s and early 1990s to permit families more choice in the public schools to which they sent their children. This trend was designed to break the assignment of children to public schools based exclusively on their residential location. The school choice movement gained increasing prominence throughout the 1990s, as states across the United States augmented their school choice laws with charter school laws. Today, charter schools are a well-accepted part of the broader public school ecosystem in the United States. As public schools, they allow families to actively choose where to enrol their children without resorting to paying private school fees. Mintrom hypothesized that policy entrepreneurs constitute an identifiable class of political actors whose presence and actions can significantly raise the probability of legislative consideration and approval of policy innovations. He tested this hypothesis by exploring the contextualized work of school choice policy entrepreneurs.

Like Schneider and Teske (1992), Mintrom used a survey to identify policy entrepreneurs and their activities in support of school choice. The survey questionnaire made significant demands for expert knowledge and judgement on the part of the recipients. For all states, the chief state school officer was asked to nominate the best person in his or her organization to answer the questions. Copies were also sent to the governor's advisor on education policy in each state and representatives of the state affiliates of the major teachers unions. Questionnaires were also sent to academics with a reputation for knowledge of their state school finance systems, members of state policy think tanks known to have an interest in education reform and members of the grass-roots organization Citizens for Educational Freedom. The responses included at least two from every state. In twenty-six states, survey respondents identified individuals who they considered matched the description of being policy entrepreneurs. A range of follow-up approaches were taken to ensure that the policy entrepreneurs identified were, indeed, knowledgeable advocates of school choice who had been active for several years in each state. These included conducting interviews with some of the individuals identified as policy entrepreneurs.

In baseline models designed to predict initial legislative consideration and subsequent legislative adoption of school choice, Mintrom (1997b) used measures of school system characteristics, key features of state politics and a state-to-state innovation diffusion measure as explanatory variables. The baseline legislative consideration model revealed that consideration of school choice was less likely in state house election years and when opposition from teachers' unions was strong. Legislative consideration of school choice in neighbouring states made legislative consideration of school choice more likely. In the baseline adoption model, legislative adoption of school choice was more likely when average high school student scores on standard aptitude tests were declining. Adoption was less likely when union opposition was strong.

Mintrom augmented these baseline models with two others. The first added a variable indicating the presence of school choice policy entrepreneurs. The second added a variable indicating the abilities of the policy entrepreneurs in several activities: problem framing, team leadership and the use of policy networks. In all models, these variables indicated that the presence of policy entrepreneurs has a strong impact on the likelihood that policy change will be considered and adopted. Further, as expected, the abilities of the policy entrepreneurs mattered. Those who were more adept at problem framing, team leadership and the use of policy networks were able to significantly raise the likelihood that school choice would gain legislative consideration and be adopted into law.

This study of policy entrepreneurs operating at the state level in the United States provided systematic evidence of the important role they play in getting innovative policy ideas onto government agendas and securing legislative change. Of course, policy entrepreneurs, like other actors in the policymaking process, must be aware of the constraints imposed by election cycles and interest-group opposition to their proposals. But many possibilities remain for policy entrepreneurs to form relationships and to develop arguments for the purpose of improving their chances of securing policy change.

These findings provided systematic evidence on the impact policy entrepreneurs could have on policymaking. Still, that raised new questions about exactly *how* policy entrepreneurs act so as to have such an impact. In the same research project, Mintrom subsequently explored the uses policy entrepreneurs make of networking, coalition building and the creation of local demonstration projects. Mintrom (2000) presents the overall set of explorations and findings. Research by other scholars has contributed further evidence concerning the impact that policy entrepreneurs can have in promoting policy change (e.g., Drummond 2010; Feiock and Bae 2011; Huitema, Lebel and Meijerink 2011). In addition, in recent years, many scholars have explored strategies adopted by policy entrepreneurs to advance their advocacy activities. The relevant studies have employed a variety of research designs. We next consider key insights from a selection of those studies.

4.3 Exploring the Effectiveness of Specific Strategies

Policy entrepreneurs are known to use a variety of strategies to secure support for their policy goals. In Section 1, we listed seven common ones: (1) thinking strategically, (2) framing problems, (3) building teams, (4) using and expanding networks; (5) working with advocacy coalitions, (6) leading by example and (7) scaling-up advocacy efforts and supporting policy change. We return now to a selection of those strategies – framing problems, using and expanding networks, and leading by example. Our interest centres on how policy entrepreneurs match strategies to contexts and what researchers have discovered about the effectiveness of such activities, as judged by observed impacts. The recent studies discussed here usefully illustrate the variety of methods now being used to study policy entrepreneurs, the strategies they use, the contexts they operate in and the impacts of their actions. Those methods include analysis of geodata, network analysis and historical institutional analysis.

4.3.1 Framing Problems

Policy entrepreneurs can often advance their goals through careful interpretation and portrayal of the current situation. Such actions, broadly construed as 'problem framing', are always political. They involve assembling new evidence and the making of novel arguments, all with the intention of changing political alignments and, hence, the status quo (see, e.g., Dewulf and Bouwen 2012; Mintrom and Luetjens 2017.)

Here, I discuss a study by Ilana Shpaizman and her colleagues, which shows how policy entrepreneurs worked to increase Jewish land ownership in the conflict-ridden Holy Basin of Jerusalem between 1981 and 2013 (Shpaizman, Swed and Pedahzur 2016). This part of Jerusalem lies at the heart of continuing Palestinian and Israeli disputes over land use, occupation and control. As the authors note, around the Temple of the Mount matters have been known to get 'so sensitive that the prime minister's formal approval is required to remove the trash' (p. 1055). Despite the heightened tensions in this region, the policy entrepreneurs involved sought to advance Jewish control over large areas of land, expanding the permanent Jewish Israeli foothold in the Holy Basin. They met with considerable success.

This case illustrates the application of various strategies, including thinking strategically and team building. But it is the deliberate framing (or reframing) of specific practices that stands out. These practices, combined with incremental 'inch by inch' work within current legislative arrangements, were undertaken with the purpose of achieving 'gradual transformative change'. The case also shows what can be gained by carefully exploiting every margin of existing policy settings. This can be especially helpful when other approaches to securing policy change seem all but impossible. Exploiting every margin within the status quo can be helpful as a means for moving towards desired outcomes before embarking on more extensive advocacy efforts.

In presenting this case of problem reframing, Shpaizman and her colleagues call it 'conversion'. They define 'conversion' as 'redirecting existing policies to new ends beyond their initial intent' (p. 1046). Specially, they show how quiet and legal (albeit ethically questionable) exploitation of current laws allowed land acquisition that would not have been possible by other means. The acquisitions involved highly strategic use of bureaucratic processes. In one set of cases, they occurred through exploitation of ambiguities in an absentee property law. In another, the acquisitions occurred through exploitation of procedures intended to protect antiquities discovered during routine construction work.

Shpaizman and her colleagues described this as a 'least likely' case of policy entrepreneurship. Taken on its face, nothing about the facts of the situation would lead us to expect the observed outcome, simply because the forces supporting the status quo in property ownership and control were so strong. The researchers used various documents and geodata on the urban settlement expansion of the Israeli Jewish population in the Holy Basin to determine how the policy entrepreneurs pursued their goals, and their level of success. They suggest problem framing was critical. It involved changing the focus of discussion, shifting the venue to quiet bureaucrat business as usual and working to build cooperative relations with key government officials.

4.3.2 Using and Expanding Networks

Policy entrepreneurs understand that their networks of contacts represent repositories of skills and knowledge which they can draw on to support their initiatives (Burt 2000; Knoke 1990; Mintrom and Vergari 1998). Early research on policy entrepreneurs and policy networks revealed that engagement in cross-jurisdictional networks can help policy entrepreneurs amass the kind of evidence they need to convince decision makers that a proposed change is attractive and effective. Meanwhile, engagement in networks in and around government in their home jurisdictions is vital for gaining legislative adoption (Mintrom and Vergari 1998). During recent decades, significant advances have been made in network analysis and its application within political science and policy studies (see, e.g., Lubell et al. 2012; Yi and Scholz 2015). This has laid the foundations for exciting new explorations of the location of policy entrepreneurs within networks and how network connections support their advocacy efforts. For example, through their use of network analysis, Dimitris Christopoulos and Karin Ingold (2015) refined our understanding of the strategies that policy entrepreneurs use to gain support in policy communities. Network analysis is conducive to capturing power relations, as it can be used to explore how information is shared, how reputations are developed and how support builds among actors in and around policymaking venues. Network analysis also opens opportunities for blending insights from qualitative and quantitative evidence and triangulating findings attained using multiple analytical approaches.

Gwen Arnold, Le Anh Nguyen Long and Madeline Gottlieb (2017) applied a sophisticated approach to network analysis to explore how policy entrepreneurs in the state of New York engaged in advocacy efforts regarding high-volume hydraulic fracturing. This is a noteworthy study because it exploited the potential for using quantitative analysis that comes from focusing on political action at the local-government level. They followed Mark Schneider and Paul Teske's (1992) method of approaching city clerks for information on the activities of policy entrepreneurs. In so doing, they explicitly explored the actions of both policy entrepreneurs who supported high-volume hydraulic fracturing and policy entrepreneurs who opposed it. This allowed them to compare and contrast how policy entrepreneurs from different sides of this controversial issue made use of their network connections to enhance their political advocacy. Further, through carefully gathering and subsequently analysing a large set of media reports mentioning the policy entrepreneurs of interest, Arnold and her colleagues were able to derive a range of fresh insights concerning the socially embedded nature of policy entrepreneurship.

Through their study of policy entrepreneurs and municipal decision-making about high-volume hydraulic fracturing, Arnold and her colleagues reached several useful conclusions. First, they found that policy entrepreneurs who enjoyed a larger coalition of allied interests in the relevant municipal governance network tended to attain more policy success. This finding is consistent with much of the scholarship on advocacy coalitions that has emerged over recent decades. Second, those who sought to upset the status quo – which typically meant those opposed to fracturing – benefitted from being able to access and deploy novel, policy-relevant information and resources. By doing so, they were better able to challenge the pro-economic development interests that often dominate local government. Finally, these researchers found that policy entrepreneurs who supported fracturing tended to have an easier time in their advocacy efforts. They were able to achieve their policy goals mainly by engaging directly with local government decision makers. That is because they were typically seeking to maintain the status quo. They had less need for new and novel information, and could focus their energies on staying close to those with power. In contrast, those who sought to upset the status quo needed to maintain strong network ties both into local government and out to broader activist communities.

4.3.3 Leading by Example

Risk aversion among decision makers presents a major challenge for actors seeking to promote significant policy change. In response, policy entrepreneurs often take actions intended to reduce opposition to change. A common strategy involves engaging with others to establish demonstration projects or other 'facts on the ground'. Such leadership by example has been used by policy entrepreneurs in a range of settings. A useful case is offered by Tulia G. Falleti (2010) in her work on policy entrepreneurs in the Brazilian healthcare system, who were active within a militarized and repressive political system from the early 1970s until the late 1980s.

It is generally accepted that health reforms introduced in Brazil's 1988 constitution and implemented throughout the 1990s were the result of a critical juncture, marked by the transition to democracy. However, Falleti documents how these health reforms actually represented the culmination of a gradual set of changes. These began long before the transition to democracy. Actors on the periphery of the existing system drove the change process. The opening for the strategies of these 'subversives' was provided by the military rulers. In the 1970s, the military introduced healthcare reforms to solidify authoritarian rule by extending the state's presence to the countryside. In response, the 'subversives', known in Brazil as the *Senitarista* movement, sought to make the Brazilian healthcare policy more universal and less centralized. When they were blocked by powerful federal players, they redoubled their local experimentation, focusing on preventive healthcare initiatives, including the promotion of public sanitation initiatives. Strengthened by the gradual process of political opening and democratization, the policy entrepreneurs in the *Senitarista* movement imprinted their healthcare model across the system. The reforms of 1988 revealed – and also codified and institutionalized – the principles of decentralization and universalism that had already been advanced such that they were assuming a dominant role in the system. By acting at the local level and starting their initiatives in remote parts of the country, these policy entrepreneurs faced less opposition and could more readily build coalitions of support for their actions. Taking advantage of cracks in the system, they built small preventive care and sanitation stations. Over time, these expanded to more localities, and then across states, eventually establishing the basis for a health system that was more universal and decentralized overall.

Falleti's case offers a good example of policy entrepreneurs leading change within a system, but in local or remote areas, removed from the centres of power. Their initiatives served both to prefigure and lay the groundwork for subsequent broad-based change. Those changes had the effect of extending quality healthcare to the poor. They produced significant improvements in healthcare outcomes across the country in subsequent decades. Infant mortality rates declined and life expectancy rates increased dramatically.

4.4 Exploring Dynamic Change

When scholars began documenting the activities of policy entrepreneurs, they tended to focus on their efforts to promote specific legislative changes. John Kingdon's (1984 [2011]) explication of the actions of policy entrepreneurs around the policymaking process in Washington, DC offers a classic example. The emergence of quantitative research interpreting contexts and assessing impacts opened the way for exploring dynamic change. Could the actions of policy entrepreneurs in one jurisdiction inspire others to pursue similar policy goals elsewhere? Michael Mintrom's (1997b) study of policy entrepreneurs operating at the state-government level across the United States was deliberately intended to assess the degree to which policy entrepreneurship supported the wider diffusion of policy innovations. Prior to that study, discussions of policy diffusion assumed cross-state information flows facilitated the spread of policy ideas. Yet little attention had been paid to how those information flows operated. Mintrom's focus on policy entrepreneurs and their engagement in broader policy networks presented a plausible, political explanation of policy diffusion patterns.

Paying close attention to the actions of policy entrepreneurs opens the way to explain how policy innovations might catch on and rapidly diffuse across whole political systems. If, like Scott Kalafatis and Maria Carmen Lemos (2017), we can show that policy entrepreneurs are more likely to be active in metropolitan regions characterized by many small, fragmented local governments, then it seems plausible to suggest that policy entrepreneurs in one such local jurisdiction can inspire similar actions by like-minded actors in nearby jurisdictions. If, like Gwen Arnold, Le Anh Nguyen Long and Madeline Gottlieb (2017), we can show being embedded in rich information networks can assist policy entrepreneurs attain specific policy goals, then it seems plausible to suggest that those networks act as vital conduits for the spread of policy ideas. If, like Tulia G. Falleti (2010), we can show how – over many years – like-minded, networked policy entrepreneurs established and replicated specific practices across regions of a country, building coalitions of supporters as they did so, then it seems plausible to suggest that those practices were the blueprint for reforms ultimately enacted at the national level.

Exploring dynamic change calls for research designs that allow for comparison across multiple cases. However, such research designs need not conform to the rigours of sophisticated quantitative analysis in order to make valuable contributions. So long as the work is theory-driven, and is strongly informed by earlier contributions, then the potential exists for such work to advance our knowledge of the connections between policy entrepreneurship and dynamic change. In that respect, work by Nissim Cohen and his colleagues has extended our understanding of the ripple effects that policy entrepreneurs can have across broader systems.

Tamar Arieli and Nissim Cohen (2013) explored how policy entrepreneurs can promote post-conflict normalization of cross-country trade and cooperation. Using the case of the Israel–Jordan border after the two countries signed a historic peace treaty in 1994, Arieli and Cohen sought to document the activities of policy entrepreneurs who were motivated to establish positive cross-border engagements. In the process, they noted that multiple policy entrepreneurs representing different sectors of society took significant and early steps to normalize cross-border interactions. In all cases, the policy entrepreneurs acted as 'first movers'. Their actions to establish productive relations with cross-border counterparts had powerful demonstration effects. They showed that cross-border cooperation was not just desirable, but possible. Their actions influenced the actions of many others. Even more importantly, those early entrepreneurial actions served to reinforce on the ground the spirit of the peace treaty. Ultimately, they were much more important to symbolizing and maintaining peace than the thousands of colourful balloons released at the end of the 1994 treaty-signing ceremony.

In conceptually related work, Doron Navot and Nissim Cohen (2015) explored how policy entrepreneurs have been able to reduce corruption in Israel. Again, this is a theory-driven study that makes effective use of in-depth case studies. For our purposes it is important work because it directly speaks to the claim that policy entrepreneurs can have system-changing impacts through the influence of their actions. In this work, Navot and Cohen explored the activities of two of the most dominant anticorruption entrepreneurs in Israel. They showed that these two individuals, in their distinctive ways, deployed many of the strategies that we have noted as often being used by policy entrepreneurs. For example, they built formal and informal networks that provided them with the contacts they needed to accomplish their anticorruption goals. In the process, they exhibited a strong commitment to fostering anti-corruption measures. They initiated formal mechanisms to reduce corrupt practices, such as promotion of legislative changes or pursuit of specific judicial decisions. They also worked at building their reputations as honest brokers for informants and insiders. They subsequently used verifiable information obtained from these sources to promote scandals. Crucially, Navot and Cohen note that, even when these policy entrepreneurs were unsuccessful in securing policy change, they reduced the prevalence of corruption across Israel by raising public consciousness and increasing the level of scrutiny into corrupt practices. Such action created uncertainty in the broader political context, deterring those considering abusing their power. In short, these policy entrepreneurs had honed the skill of creating ripple effects across the political system.

All of us have attended events in large arenas, such as football games, where everyone can talk or shout as much as they like, knowing they will be heard by only a handful of people around them. But when a speaker commands a microphone connected to the sound system, they will quickly become the centre of attention, and everyone will hear their message. Policy entrepreneurs face choices. They can be like everyone else and voice their thoughts to a handful of people, or they can find ways to amplify their voice, and gain the attention of many people. Ultimately, the policy entrepreneurs who command that broader attention are the ones who should be of most interest to scholars of public policy and political science. They make up an important subset of the people Steve Jobs once famously hailed as 'the crazy ones'. In Jobs' words: 'You can quote them, disagree with them, glorify or vilify them, but the only thing you can't do is ignore them because they change things' (Jobs, 1997). Policy entrepreneurs are bold. They take risks that many others – including many elected politicians – would not take. So, to appropriate from Steve Jobs, I say of policy entrepreneurs: 'The ones who are crazy enough to think that they can change the world are the ones who do.' Given their capability to have broad influence, it is appropriate for political scientists and those who study policy-making processes to pay serious attention to how this unique class of political actors can drive dynamic change.

4.5 Conclusion

Due to a series of carefully designed research projects conducted from the early 1990s onwards, a cumulative set of insights have emerged concerning policy entrepreneurs. We now have a sound appreciation of how contextual conditions can raise or lower the chances that policy entrepreneurs will emerge to address significant collective action problems. When the venues for political action are somewhat harder to access and when relevant interest groups are active and powerful, it becomes harder for policy entrepreneurs to make a difference. We saw how evidence provided by Mark Schneider and Paul Teske supports the view that entrepreneurial actors are driven by incentives. They are less likely to emerge on the political scene when the chances of making a difference seem low. Other studies have further supported that view. Michael Mintrom's work from the 1990s, building on the work of Schneider and Teske, provided systematic evidence of the impact that policy entrepreneurs can have on driving policy change. Even so, that work made clear just how important context is to the success or otherwise of policy entrepreneurs. Subsequent studies, noted here, have greatly advanced our under-standing of how specific strategies assist policy entrepreneurs in achieving their policy goals. A particularly important aspect of policy entrepreneurship is the potential that it has to drive change across multiple jurisdictions. How can we account for dynamic policy change? Several of the studies discussed in this section have advanced our knowledge of broader policy change processes and the role that policy entrepreneurs can play in the diffusion of policy innovations.

This stock take of the trajectory of research on policy entrepreneurs, contexts and impacts has set the stage for discussing how this highly fruitful line of scholarship might best be continued. The next section offers insights in that regard. The motivating question is how future studies of policy entrepreneur-ship and dynamic change might generate new insights into the nature of con-temporary politics.

5 Directions for Future Research

Research on policy entrepreneurs has burgeoned over the past three decades. In that time, policy entrepreneurs have gone from a handful of mentions in isolated case studies to many detailed assessments grounded in sophisticated research designs. Along the way, various attempts have been made to draw connections between the localized actions of specific policy entrepreneurs and the emergence of broader, system-level policy changes. That micro-to-macro connection deserves ongoing investigation. Through such research, the possibility builds for the actor-centred analysis of policy entrepreneurship to advance our understanding of structure and agency. Indeed, a fully realised, theory-driven programme of research on policy entrepreneurs could explain much about dynamic change. In the process, it could generate profound insights regarding change processes in contemporary politics, from the local level to the global.

This section explores directions for future research on policy entrepreneurs, the contexts in which they operate, the strategies they deploy and the impacts they have. Throughout, consideration is given to how such research could extend from previous work. Typically, previous investigations of policy entrepreneurs have explored their emergence and actions within specific policy domains and contexts. For example, various studies have considered the work of policy entrepreneurs operating in and around subnational government to promote policy innovations designed to reduce the release of greenhouse gases (e.g., Drummond 2010; Kalafatis and Lemos 2017; Mintrom and Luetjens 2017; Rabe 2004). Focusing on specific policy domains and contexts has worked well in terms of generating new insights regarding policy entrepreneurship. Our existing knowledge of policy entrepreneurs and dynamic change has accumulated through a variety of research approaches. Those contemplating future research on policy entrepreneurship would do well to keep an open mind about what approaches might serve them best. Historical case studies, comparative case studies, quantitative time series, event history modelling, survey-based research and network analyses have all contributed to knowledge development. Room exists for use of new methods, some of which will be discussed here. So long as it is theory-driven, all forms of empirical research can be broadly cumulative in nature. That has been the story so far in the research on policy entrepreneurs.

As further research is conducted, a question of audience arises. Is such work intended primarily to advance scholarly knowledge of policy entrepreneurship, policy innovation and the mechanisms of dynamic policy change? Or is it intended mainly to be of practical relevance to would-be policy entrepreneurs, people in and around government seeking to develop and promote policy innovations in pursuit of significant change? In this regard, I generally subscribe to the view that the best insights for practice will emerge from theory-driven, systematic empirical work. Of course, I acknowledge that translation of insights from such work does not always occur. Further, those seeking to be policy entrepreneurs are likely to gain many vital insights into effective practice through 'learning by doing' and by taking advice from other experienced practitioners. But if we are to seriously push ahead both in understanding policy entrepreneurship and encouraging effective practice, then primacy must be given to theory-driven, systematic empirical work. In the absence of careful research, we are left with a collection of anecdotes. And the problem with anecdote is that all questions about how to proceed in any given set of circumstances will be prefaced by the rather unsatisfying disclaimer that 'it all depends'. We can – and must – do better than that.

5.1 Policy Entrepreneurs as a Distinct Class of Actors

John Kingdon memorably observed that policy entrepreneurs 'could be in or out of government, in elected or appointed positions, in interest groups or research organizations. But their defining characteristic, much as in the case of a business entrepreneur, is their willingness to invest their resources – time, energy, reputation, and sometimes money – in the hope of a future return' (1984 [2011], p. 122). Here, Kingdon asserted that policy entrepreneurs represent a distinct class of actors. They are different from typical elected politicians, typical appointed officials, typical interest group leaders and so on. Since Kingdon made that observation, a fair degree of effort has gone into understanding what it is that makes policy entrepreneurs different from other actors in and around policymaking circles. That effort has produced a convergence of views on the distinctive characteristics of policy entrepreneurs. Meanwhile, no attempts have been made to discredit these claims that policy entrepreneurs comprise a distinct class of actors.

As researchers have sought to better define the notion of the entrepreneurial actor in and around policymaking circles, a significant amount of borrowing has occurred from studies of entrepreneurship in the world of business (see, e.g., Arieli and Cohen 2013; Mintrom 2000, Petridou 2016). When introducing their studies, researchers typically note common attributes of policy entrepreneurs. Those attributes tend to match up with those introduced and discussed in Section 1. That is, policy entrepreneurs are claimed to exhibit ambition, social acuity, credibility, sociability and tenacity. Good reasons can be given for proposing a list like this. Yet it is also noteworthy that such attributes would serve anyone well who wishes to get ahead in life and have an impact on the world around them. Exhibiting these attributes, in and of itself, does not make someone entrepreneurial.

How might future research improve our confidence that the people we identify as policy entrepreneurs fit within a distinctive class of political actors? First, we must accept that all policy entrepreneurs will likely have other identities – elected politician, appointed official, business professional, interest group leader, activist or concerned citizen. So we should not seek to identify a mutually exclusive class of political actors. Indeed, some exciting recent work has been explicitly exploring the overlaps in the identities of policy entrepreneurs and other classes of political actors. See, for example, Nissim Cohen's work with colleagues on street-level bureaucrats and policy entrepreneurship (Frisch-Aviram, Cohen and Beeri 2018) and Marijn Faling's work with colleagues on policy entrepreneurs as boundary spanners (Faling et al. 2018). More of such work could assist us in exploring what is unique to the identity of policy entrepreneurs. Second, we need to find ways to measure the hypothesized 'entrepreneurial attributes'. Ideally, this measurement would be done in a comparative way. We should be able to compare both *among* individuals deemed policy entrepreneurs and *between* policy entrepreneurs and other political actors operating in similar contexts.

Suppose we sought to identify political actors who have been promoting improved means of helping unemployed people retrain and find work. We might surmise that these actors are operating predominantly at the state level in a federal government system (e.g., the United States or Australia). Following past research, we could use survey research to identify these people. We could ask knowledgeable people in the employment policy domain to name people who have been promoting such policy change. Let us further suppose that this survey work generates for us a list of fifteen names of people spread across five jurisdictions. At this point, it would be useful to measure relevant attributes of these fifteen individuals, with the goal of determining the extent to which each of them seems to approximate current notions of the identity of a policy entrepreneur. This is a common strategy that has been used in the past. It can be combined with a range of approaches to 'verify' that the identified individuals have been key players in promoting the desired policy change. A more powerful strategy would involve taking a further step. It would require measuring the same relevant attributes in other political actors matched by context to the fifteen individuals identified as policy entrepreneurs.

While adding a level of complexity to the research project, this step would allow us to compare the attributes of the purported policy entrepreneurs with those of other political actors operating in their local contexts. From here, we could gain new insights into the extent to which policy entrepreneurs really are distinctive with respect to attributes like ambition, social acuity and tenacity. Whatever the findings, they could assist us to think more clearly about the factors that contribute to observed policy successes on the part of policy entrepreneurs. We could, for example, start to specify the relative extent to which the success of policy entrepreneurs is due to personal attributes, relevant features of the local policymaking context or the effective use of strategies.

5.2 Policy Entrepreneurship in Context

When John Kingdon (1984 [2011]) discussed the work of policy entrepreneurs, he did so within a broader theory of the policymaking process. His multiple streams approach explicitly acknowledges the fundamental role contextual conditions play in filtering options for policy change. Recent and emerging political episodes provide one set of contextual filters, the emergence and discussion of problems provide another set, and conversations in and around policymaking circles provide more filters. That is not to say that context determines everything. Policy entrepreneurs with high levels of social acuity can often perceive windows of opportunity where others would not. They can also use their social acuity to figure out what kinds of arguments would work best in allowing them to bring their ideas for policy change to prominence on the broader political agenda.

Over the past few decades, research on policy entrepreneurs has become increasingly sophisticated in taking account of how factors in their operating contexts can influence the degree of success that policy entrepreneurs achieve as they work to promote policy change. At the most general level, studies of policy entrepreneurship should always seek to address three questions about context. First, what are the most significant political, social and/or economic factors that have established this context? Second, what actors and interests tend to have most influence in this context, and why is that? Third, assuming no policy entrepreneurs were present, in what ways, if any, might the status quo have shifted anyway? Those studying policy entrepreneurs can gain many insights into context by interpreting them with reference to established theories of the policymaking process (see Section 3). When beginning an investigation of policy entrepreneurship, elite theory signposts us to think hard about the constellation of interests present, and how that constellation evolved. This can lead to consideration of current institutional arrangements, the forces that shaped their development and how those current arrangements advance the interests of some groups to the detriment of others. The theory of incrementalism leads us to consider dynamics within the current policymaking process, as does the theory of punctuated equilibrium. Both theories encourage us to think about policy change across a period of time leading to the present. In this, they share a point of commonality with the Advocacy Coalition Framework, which likewise enjoins us to explore stability and change in relationships among relevant interest groups and policymaking communities over time. Looking ahead, much scope exists for those who study policy entrepreneurship to be more creative in their engagements with theories of the policymaking process. Theoretical treatments of policy processes are continuously evolving. Explorations of policy entrepreneurship should evolve with them. In that regard, there is considerable potential for studies of policy entrepreneurship to be informed by recent developments in the narrative policy framework (see, e.g., Kirkpatrick and Stoutenborough 2018).

Beyond these considerations of ways to advance our understanding of policy entrepreneurs within policymaking processes, there are various ways that we could deepen our knowledge of policy entrepreneurship in context. Here, four possibilities will be discussed. They concern: (1) the other identities of policy entrepreneurs – picking up on a matter touched upon earlier in this section; (2) the steps in policymaking processes where policy entrepreneurs choose to be most active; (3) how policy entrepreneurs emerge and position themselves given the multiple levels upon which governments operate and, finally, (4) the emergence of policy entrepreneurs in non-Western political environments.

It has long been argued that policy entrepreneurs can operate from a range of positions in and around government. Many studies produced over the past three decades corroborate this view. However, now that our understanding of the work of policy entrepreneurs has evolved, there would be merit in considering more closely how specific contexts might serve to shape and constrain the kinds of actors who emerge as policy entrepreneurs in relation to specific policy issues. For example, we might anticipate that people with backgrounds in teaching or in serving as school principals might be found leading efforts to change specific aspects of education policy. Likewise, we might anticipate that medical specialists might sometimes become policy entrepreneurs in the arena of health policy. But surely it would be a surprise to find either an educator or a medical specialist playing a prominent role in policy debates regarding mechanisms for the distribution of water rights among farmers. Substantive knowledge gives participants credibility in policymaking processes. Therefore, we should be able to say more about how contextual factors serve to filter the kinds of people who emerge as policy entrepreneurs, and the skills and experiences they bring to policy debates. By the same logic, we should be able to give an account of conditions that favour the emergence of elected politicians as policy entrepreneurs, or senior bureaucrats, or interest group representatives. Equally, we should be able to account for why engaged citizens can emerge as policy entrepreneurs in some contexts but are rarely found in others.

Previous research on policy entrepreneurs has tended to focus on their attempts to promote policy innovations so that they gain prominence on government agendas. In such studies, the adoption of a new policy within a given jurisdiction is treated as the end point of advocacy efforts. But is it? Given the high degree of variation that has long been observed in the effectiveness with which public policies are implemented (Howlett and Ramesh 2016), it would appear that many opportunities exist for policy entrepreneurs to be highly influential during policy implementation processes. For example, space exists in many systems for effective practices in one location to be emulated in others (Meier and O'Toole 2001). Given the potential power of programme evaluations to contribute to changing perceptions of policy effectiveness (Baumgartner and Jones 1993; Carter and Jacobs 2014), it is also reasonable to assume that some policy entrepreneurship might actually start with evaluation work. While there are certainly examples of policy entrepreneurs making their mark through policy implementation (Arieli and Cohen 2013; Sugiyama 2011), more research would be welcome here, including research on how policy entrepreneurs use programme evaluations as tools for agenda setting. Ultimately, we could benefit from accounts of policy entrepreneurship that explain why, given specific contextual conditions, it made sense for policy entrepreneurs to start their advocacy efforts in the ways that they did.

Functional reasons can readily be found to explain why national governments tend to take charge of foreign policy, trade and defence arrangements, while local governments focus on public transport, traffic and trash. Yet, we also know that many areas of public policy defy simple functional classifications. In federal systems of government, it is common to see national, state and local governments all weighing in to policy discussions regarding public schooling, public health and aspects of environmental policy. This is true for many other areas of public policy as well. Studies of policy entrepreneurship have explored the pursuit of policy change at all levels of government – national, state and local. However, only a handful have explored the dynamics between these levels of government. For example, Michael Mintrom (1997a) considered the state-local nexus in policy innovation. The focus there was on how policy entrepreneurs might promote change at the local level as a way to encourage state legislators to adopt similar changes on a broader scale. Similarly, Michael Mintrom and Joannah Luetjens (2017) noted how policy entrepreneurs worked at the local level to promote climate change mitigation strategies. In a similar vein, Barry Rabe (2004) demonstrated how state governors in the United States were promoting policies to mitigate climate change in the absence of such initiatives coming out of Washington DC. We believe that much could be learned from further exploration of the jurisdictions in which policy entrepreneurs choose to pursue specific policy agendas, and why those jurisdictions are chosen. Frank Baumgartner and Bryan Jones (1993) have referred to this as 'venue shopping'. The logic of venue shopping among policy entrepreneurs deserves further examination.

Finally, it is exciting to see research on policy entrepreneurship increasingly being conducted around the globe. For example, recent case studies from China indicate that policy entrepreneurship occurs there, even though the political system is very different from the political system in the United States, where the notion of policy entrepreneurship was first coined (Hammond 2013; He 2018; Teets 2015). Looking ahead, further investigation of policy entrepreneurship in a diversity of policymaking contexts promises two benefits. First, it could serve to illuminate advocacy practices in a range of jurisdictions in a fashion that is novel and that potentially offers new insights on political processes within those jurisdictions. Second, from the perspective of theory development, these expanding attempts to study policy entrepreneurship open space for richer consideration of many of the points already made throughout this section. That is to say, these emerging studies will allow for more comparative assessment of how contextual factors shape the emergence, attributes, actions and impacts of policy entrepreneurs.

5.3 The Strategies of Policy Entrepreneurs

Earlier, we considered how further research could advance our understanding of policy entrepreneurs as a distinct class of actors. Here, we consider how future research could advance our understanding of when, how and with what impact, policy entrepreneurs deploy specific strategies. While policy entrepreneurs seem unique political actors in the sense of seeking to promote policy change, they are not unique in the strategies that they often deploy. Earlier, I claimed that we could gain more appreciation of the attributes of policy entrepreneurs by studying policy entrepreneurs in comparison with other political actors. Here, I suggest that we could likewise sharpen our understanding of policy entrepreneurs as strategic actors through explicit acknowledgement of the commonalities between the specific strategies they use and the strategies that other actors in and around politics and policymaking use. To acknowledge and more carefully explore this overlap in the practices of various strategic actors could be seen as challenging the unique status ascribed to policy entrepreneurs in the extant literature. That is not the intent. Rather, starting with the assumption that all actors in politics, policymaking and related fields use specific strategies provides a stronger empirical basis upon which to assert the uniqueness of how policy entrepreneurs deploy those strategies.

Thomas Kalil (2017) documented how he and others working in the White House emulated common strategies of policy entrepreneurship to good effect in advancing their proposals for policy innovation. His list is insightful and would be of benefit to anyone working in organizational settings. The bottom line is that, if you want to have influence, you have to carefully manage many things. For example, there are typically actions all of us can take to make it easier for others to agree with us and lend support to our proposals for change. For my own part, I have long claimed that there are a number of 'people skills' that policy analysts can usefully deploy (Mintrom 2003). My decision to write at length about those skills was initially motivated by my understanding that many people engaged in policy development could improve their performance by acting like policy entrepreneurs. Yet, an even better starting place would be to acknowledge the broad applicability of thinking strategically (see, e.g., Dixit and Nalebuff 2008), and then explore the extent to which policy entrepreneurs deploy specific strategies that all rational actors could benefit from using. Taking that approach, we would avoid the trap of assuming that the set of strategies that policy entrepreneurs use is fixed. Rather, we could continually investigate what strategies policy entrepreneurs appear to use, and work to explain why they do so.

Over the past couple of decades, various research contributions have been made with the intention of further explicating specific strategies used by policy entrepreneurs. Consequently, we now know a reasonable amount about how policy entrepreneurs utilize problem framing, how they establish teams to advance their policy goals, their use of networks and their place within advocacy coalitions. Looking to the future, additional contributions exploring the use of these specific strategies could advance our knowledge of policy entrepreneurship. While, to date, a fair amount of quantitative work has been done to explore the ways policy entrepreneurs operate within networks, most other common strategies have been explored through case studies. More insights could come from systematic exploration of questions such as: What strategies do policy entrepreneurs use? When do they use them? Why, and to what effect? And how do their uses of particular strategies make them similar to or different from other actors in and around the policymaking process? Sound research addressing these questions could contribute both to our knowledge of policy entrepreneurship and, potentially, to our broader awareness of how specific strategies are used within policymaking circles.

Aside from contributing to curiosity-driven research on policy entrepreneurship, studying the strategies of policy entrepreneurs holds the promise of yielding insights for those who aspire to be policy entrepreneurs. Avinash Dixit and Barry Nalebuff (2008) wrote their primer on strategic thinking to help people training for professional careers. Thomas Kalil (2017) produced his reflections on policy entrepreneurship in the White House also with the intention of passing on useful advice to other would-be influencers. All of which raises a fundamental question: Can policy entrepreneurship be taught? Contributions to the literature on expertise and its development suggest that most skills can be taught, although how well they will be embedded in the practices of individuals will come down to differences in both aptitude and motivation (see, e.g., Deci and Ryan 1985; Ericsson, Prietula and Cokely 2007; Mintrom 2014). Many efforts have been made to impart business skills, leadership skills and skills in creativity. Likewise, there is a thriving literature on how to train people to be effective entrepreneurs (e.g., Brannback and Carsrud 2015; Margolit and Kopp 2019). Looking to the future, it would be terrific to see scholars with knowledge of policy entrepreneurship translating that into practical advice for those seeking to driving policy innovations and dynamic change.

5.4 Assessing Impact

Policy entrepreneurs appear in the literature as energetic actors who engage in collaborative action in and around government to promote significant policy change. Given that, it is appropriate to assess their impact by noting the relationship between their actions and subsequent legislative change. That has been a common analytical strategy in many contributions to the literature. Looking to the future, further research could illuminate more about the impact of policy entrepreneurs on policy change. Here, two matters are considered. First, there would be value in exploring the definition of impact. Second, building from observations made in the previous discussion of policy entrepreneurship in context, new studies could further assess the uniqueness of the contributions that policy entrepreneurs make to producing policy change. Each of these matters deserve further consideration.

Legislative change is the most public evidence that policy settings have been adjusted. Given this, the focus on legislative change as a measure of impact of policy entrepreneurs offers a plausible and objective measure of change. At the same time, as a range of studies of policy entrepreneurship have attested, other kinds of change can have important impacts and are worthy of further study. Tamar Arieli and Nissim Cohen studied how policy entrepreneurs assisted in the implementation of cross-border cooperation after the peace treaty had been signed between Israel and Jordan (Arieli and Cohen 2013). Ilana Shpaizman and her colleagues studied how policy entrepreneurs could push for change – and the impact it had – even when policy settings seemed stable. Their study illustrated how impact can happen beyond legislative change and how it can serve both to undermine current legislation and force broader policy adjustments (Shpaizman, Swed and Pedahzur 2016). In her historical institutional study of changes in healthcare policy in Brazil, Tulia Falleti showed how coordinated action across local jurisdictions could transform policies during implementation and, in the process, lay the foundations for adoption of changes in national-level policy settings (Falleti 2010). The three studies mentioned here all offer evidence of policy entrepreneurs having a significant impact that would not have been noticed if attention had been restricted to legislative change as the measure of impact. This indicates the merit in thinking more about the definition of impact and how it might shift from context to context and across points in time.

One of the nagging concerns with much of the literature on policy entrepreneurship is that policy entrepreneurs are often identified after a policy change has occurred. As a result, there is a possibility of selection bias in the research design. That is, the fact of policy change leads us to search for evidence that a policy entrepreneur was present to drive that change. Given that the change happened, the policy entrepreneur identified will be judged to have been successful. The worry is that policy entrepreneurs who are working to secure change that is yet to happen would not be identified in such research. Further, policy entrepreneurs who worked to secure change but whose efforts were defeated could also be ignored. The research design needs to look at more combinations of possibilities: Beyond the scenario with (1) policy entrepreneur present and policy change, we need to consider (2) policy entrepreneur present and no policy change, (3) no policy entrepreneur present and policy change and (4) no policy entrepreneur present and no change. Only when the full set of logical relationships between policy entrepreneurs and policy change is considered can we be more confident in any claims about the impact made by policy entrepreneurs.

Addressing the impact question in the fashion proposed here would not necessarily require a quantitative research design, but such a design would be of high value. The limitation of such research is that it calls for the study of similar policy changes across similar jurisdictions – the states of the United States, or local governments represent the sort of jurisdictional units that would support such research. Past studies working at the state level in the United States have explored impact in this way (see, e.g., Mintrom 1997b). More could be done along these lines. For example, studies have explored differences in legislation relating to apparently equivalent policy changes (see, e.g., Glick and Hays 1991; Mooney and Lee 1995). We know that a policy change, such as the introduction of charter schools in the states in the United States can range from restrictive to permissive (see, e.g., Vergari 1999). Looking to the future, there would be merit in research on policy entrepreneurs that incorporated more nuanced ways of capturing variation across jurisdictions in the scope of policy change attained. Seeking to explain that variation with reference to the actions of policy entrepreneurs could generate new insights into the relationship between the strategies used by policy entrepreneurs and the impact of those policy entrepreneurs as judged by relevant policy changes.

5.5 Policy Entrepreneurs and Dynamic Change

In the first instance, policy change has impacts within the jurisdiction where it is introduced. However, second-order impacts can be significant. This is where change in one jurisdiction serves to prompt change in other jurisdictions. Here, I describe this process as 'dynamic change'. Since the publication in 1962 of the first edition of Everett Rogers' classic, *Diffusion of Innovation*, researchers across many fields have sought to identify the factors promoting the adoption of change across communities, organizations and political jurisdictions. Influenced by Rogers, the political scientist Jack Walker explored the diffusion of policy innovation among the American states (Walker 1969). Utilizing case study methods, Nelson Polsby (1985) provided an insightful account of the politics that surround the promotion of policy innovations. In a different, but related, field, Andrew van de Ven (1986) developed an influential taxonomy of factors needed to advance innovation in organizations. This drew attention to the importance of managing attention, bringing new ideas into good currency and providing leadership in complex institutional settings. A large body of political science research has subsequently been devoted to understanding the antecedents of policy innovation diffusion (for a review, see Berry and Berry 2018). Meanwhile, a parallel body of political science research has explored the antecedents of policy transfer among nations (for a review, see Dolowitz and Marsh 1996). Some work has been made over the years to summarize the insights coming from these streams of literature (e.g., Marsh and Sharman 2009; Shipan and Volden 2008, 2012). Michael Mintrom's study of policy entrepreneurs and the diffusion of innovation deliberately sought to join the literature on policy entrepreneurship with the literature on policy innovation diffusion (Mintrom 1997b). More specifically, the claim made in that work was that policy entrepreneurs, through their involvement in policy networks, represent vital political conduits supporting dynamic change. Of course, a variety of factors serve to shape dynamic change processes.

Recent research has greatly advanced our knowledge of dynamic change. It offers a powerful platform from which future studies of policy entrepreneurs and dynamic change could build. Given the quantitative nature of this stream of research, the most fruitful future contributions will come from theory-driven quantitative empirical work. Following an extensive review of the policy diffusion literature, Charles Shipan and Craig Volden made several observations about the findings from this collective body of research (Shipan and Volden 2012). Among other things, they noted that information flows in contemporary politics are far more extensive than has ever been the case in the past. Consequently, many opportunities now exist for jurisdictions to learn from elsewhere. While there may have been a time when policy innovations appeared to spread most quickly among neighbouring jurisdictions, evidence suggests that diffusion patterns have become much more varied. Governments learn from each other, although some governments have much greater capability to do so. For example, more professional and well-resourced bureaucracies are more likely to keep up with relevant policy developments than under-resourced counterparts. Beyond that, those who adopt policy change must be convinced that it is the right thing to do. Competition among jurisdictions can often serve to prompt such change, as can coercion (e.g., higher-level governments imposing conditions on lower-level governments that force policy change).

Shipan and Volden's assessment offers important insights for those who would seek to promote dynamic policy change. First, politics matters. So, it is vital that policy entrepreneurs interpret contexts appropriately in order to determine the likely receptivity of a given jurisdiction to a policy innovation. Second, the design of the policies themselves can have a big impact on their attractiveness to would-be adopters. Complex policies spread more slowly, whereas policies compatible with current policy settings spread more quickly. The ease with which a policy innovation and its impacts elsewhere can be observed, the relative advantages it offers over the status quo and the ease with which a trial can be established all serve to enhance the likelihood that a policy innovation will spread more rapidly across jurisdictions. Further insights into processes supporting dynamic change have been offered by Gwen Arnold and her colleagues in their analysis of how networks serve to support the work of policy entrepreneurs (Arnold, Nguyen Long, and Gottlieb 2017). Those insights, too, should be of assistance to researchers seeking to further understand the work of policy entrepreneurs and how they contribute to dynamic policy change. In addition, Graeme Boushey (2010, 2012) has extended our understanding of effective means for modelling policy diffusion processes. Specifically, he has shown how insights from punctuated equilibrium theory can improve our interpretations of dynamic change processes. According to Boushey, effective framing of policy problems can increase the likelihood that they will gain the attention of policymakers, who will then be more receptive to adopting policy change. Taken together, these various recent contributions advance our understanding of dynamic change processes. They lay strong foundations for future explorations of how policy entrepreneurs drive such change.

5.6 Policy Entrepreneurs and Scaling Strategies

Our discussion to this point has considered possibilities for future research exploring the impacts of policy entrepreneurs both within specific jurisdictions and at the system-wide level. A matter worth further consideration concerns the degree to which policy entrepreneurs from the outset seek to promote system-wide change, and how that might be feasible. In Section 4, I noted Steve Jobs' famous claim that 'the ones who are crazy enough to think that they can change the world are the ones who do'. Looking to the future, with major known challenges such as climate change, technological change and world population growth, the need is great for policy solutions to be found that can be scaled to promote better environmental, social and economic outcomes. How might we explore the scaling-up of policy changes? Recently, efforts have been made to explore this matter. For example, Michael Mintrom and Madeline Thomas have considered how policy entrepreneurs might support the pursuit of the UN's Sustainable Development Goals (Mintrom and Thomas 2018). In that study, the authors noted the importance of mapping out the chains of connections that must be established between the setting of goals and the actual changing of practices on the ground that will support goal attainment. Developed further, assessment of scaling strategies would need to take into account many of the factors we have already discussed that influence policy impact and dynamic change. While sophisticated modelling work could do much to advance knowledge here, the basic mapping work is first needed, and this calls for theory-driven conceptual work, informed by observations of actual practices. In other words, the study of policy entrepreneurs and scaling strategies could currently benefit from application of a range of research strategies, from in-depth case studies to more sophisticated modelling work.

5.7 Conclusion

Research on policy entrepreneurs conducted over the past few decades has greatly advanced our understanding of this unique class of political actor and how they make change happen. That research has also laid the foundations for fruitful future work. This section has considered directions further research might take concerning the identity of policy entrepreneurs, the contexts in which they operate, the strategies they deploy and their impacts. Future research could employ various methods. Throughout this discussion, reference has been made to insights derived from, among other sources, historical case studies, comparative case studies, quantitative time series, event history modelling, survey-based research and network analyses. There is value in curiosity-driven research, because it helps us to make sense of the political world. Yet, given the many challenges faced by jurisdictions from the local to the national in the contemporary world, there are also many practical reasons why we might wish to study policy entrepreneurship. Doing so offers the prospect of improving the capabilities and effectiveness of those seeking to promote better economic, social, and environmental outcomes both in their local settings and more broadly.

6 Driving Public Policy in an Uncertain World

Since the 1980s, political scientists and scholars of public policy have contributed to a loosely constituted collective research project concerning the identification of policy entrepreneurs, what they do and the impacts they have. Research on policy entrepreneurs has explored their actions and impacts in a variety of settings across the globe. We now know quite a lot about this distinct class of political actor.

This Element began with a section discussing the kinds of political processes policy entrepreneurs initiate. Consideration was then given to what we know regarding the common political strategies policy entrepreneurs deploy in pursuit of their policy goals. This was followed by an assessment of how the concept of the policy entrepreneur intersects with traditional theories of the policymaking process. The theme of agency and structure was explored further in a discussion of how policy entrepreneur might be studied in context and how their impacts might be measured. These discussions of who policy entrepreneurs are, what they do and with what effects opened space for considering useful next steps in research on these actors who often have catalytic effects, driving dynamic change.

A speculative question motivates the discussion in this final section. What might we expect from policy entrepreneurs in the years ahead? Long ago, Heraclitus of Ephesus famously observed that change is the only constant in life. It is reasonable, then, to suggest that there is nothing new about the changing nature of our contemporary world. But *how* that change is occurring *is* new. A disconcerting feature of the present age is that we know so much more than ever before about environmental, social, political and economic processes, yet there remains so much we do not know about how best to govern elements of those processes so as to promote widely valued positive outcomes. Can policy entrepreneurs be of assistance? To address these questions, this concluding discussion further explores how policy entrepreneurs introduce new topics of policy conversation, how they create advocacy coalitions, how they show-case success and their attempts to drive dynamic change. The hope is that this discussion will prompt new thinking about how policy entrepreneurs seek to drive public policy in the face of significant uncertainty.

6.1 Promoting Policy Discussion

What is to be done? That question often serves to prompt discussions of policy development and policy change. In his analyses of entrepreneurs in the marketplace, Israel Kirzner (1973, 1997) emphasized the importance of 'alertness' and 'discovery'. Entrepreneurs, through their close engagement in market activities, come to understand what consumers desire but currently lack. This understanding guides them to bring forth desirable – and potentially profitable – innovations. In an important synthesizing project, Mark Casson (1982) emphasized the informational advantage entrepreneurs hold over others. This advantage comes from individual talent on one hand and social position of the entrepreneur on the other. It allows entrepreneurs to make 'judgemental decisions'. In this portrayal, social networks become critical resources for entrepreneurs. They channel information to the entrepreneur that can be used to identify profit opportunities (see also Casson and Giusta 2007). Together, Kirzner and Casson remind us that entrepreneurs gain valuable insights and information by being close to the market, especially to consumers. By analogy, we might say that policy entrepreneurs similarly gain valuable insights and information by being embedded in community conversations and conversations concerning public policy. John Kingdon spoke of the 'policy primeval soup' – that space where old ideas, new ideas, old issues and new issues are continuously bumping up against each other, so that new formulations might develop. With the help of insights from Kirzner and Casson, we can push this further. Policy entrepreneurs gain insights by listening and engaging with others. Some might be voicing concerns about problems in need of solutions. Some might be suggesting solutions. The genius of the policy entrepreneur often involves determining the essence of a problem and identifying a solution that is both feasible and politically acceptable. But that joining of the problem with a policy solution that is politically acceptable does not occur instantaneously. Rather, it evolves through discussion.

Policy entrepreneurs represent vital social and political agents because of their ability to promote and guide policy discussions. At their best, they are facilitative, working with others in ways that create spaces for the sharing of challenges and the mulling over of possible solutions. Looking to the future, many jurisdictions will find themselves in need of actors who can elicit the concerns and the knowledge of those around them and steer discussion towards the striking of solutions. Often, those solutions will not be novel to the situation in hand. Policy entrepreneurs or others they talk with might learn of solutions being used elsewhere, either in their own jurisdiction or further afield. The novelty emerges in the framing of the problems and the adaptation and representation of possible solutions. Getting people talking is a starting point. But it is fundamental, and it is an important contribution that policy entrepreneurs can make.

6.2 Creating Advocacy Coalitions

Policymaking is a team sport, as is policy advocacy. Therefore, while an energetic or prominent individual might often be seen as the 'face' of a specific policy innovation, policy entrepreneurs understand that they can do nothing alone. As well as being politically savvy and creative thinkers, they need to have an instinct for collaboration. This means policy entrepreneurs will often work in teams and work to establish advocacy coalitions to support their desired policy changes (Mintrom and Vergari 1996). Such coalition development need not start from scratch. Effective coalition builders work with the political alignments that are already in place and find creative ways to 'stitch up' cooperation among groups or organizations that might not have worked together before. This stitch up work often takes place through conversation. Through careful listening for what people want, and careful development of arguments, policy entrepreneurs can find ways to bring people together by identifying a common cause.

The capacity to collaborate effectively with others and to create advocacy coalitions can have significant spill-over benefits. Isolated groups and organizations that might not have been able to achieve desired policy goals on their own can gain political strength through the efforts of policy entrepreneurs. Further, by assisting others to attain desired goals, policy entrepreneurs provide evidence of progress, of forward movement. This can be extremely important, especially when most policymaking is characterized by incrementalism. Policy entrepreneurs can help others to make meaning of their advocacy work and see results. This keeps the effort to attain policy change looking realistic and worthwhile. In the absence of the catalytic work of policy entrepreneurs, a degree of political lethargy or resignation to living with the status quo could set in.

6.3 Showcasing Policy Successes

When policy innovations meet with success, many people step forwards to take credit for their introduction. Speaking of the Foreign Assistance Act of 1948, which helped rebuild much of Europe after the devastation of the Second World War, US President Harry Truman observed, 'It is amazing what you can accomplish if you do not care who gets the credit' (Truman, 1948). The Foreign Assistance Act is usually referred to as the Marshall Plan, after George Marshall, a former army general who served as US secretary of state under President Truman. But no matter who gets credit, society benefits from successful public policies. The most obvious beneficiaries are those directly affected by the policy. In the case of the Marshall Plan, that was many citizens in Europe. A less obvious, yet still vitally important benefit, is the knowledge that diffuses about the successful policy and how success happened. The Marshall Plan stood in contrast to the punitive reparations imposed on Germany in the Treaty of Versailles that formally ended the hostilities of the First World War. The general agreement that the Marshall Plan promoted sustained peace laid the foundation for subsequent donor-country funding of rebuilding work in countries emerging from war. Examples include foreign assistance to help rebuild Bosnia, Croatia, Iraq, Kuwait and Vietnam in the aftermath of war.

When policy entrepreneurs tell others about policy successes, they advance our knowledge of policy innovations, what they sought to achieve, the prevailing political conditions, what actions were necessary to attain political support and how the innovation has been implemented. This showcasing work can be done for a variety of reasons. Often, it occurs because specific policy entrepreneurs believe that they have established a new status quo that is worthy of emulation elsewhere. This kind of showcasing can be helpful. It provides evidence that advocates for policy change can use elsewhere. Further, as policy entrepreneurs 'talk up' their successes, they advertise themselves as potential 'go to' people for advice on how to make change happen. In this respect, they serve an important function in policy networks, bringing rich detail and strategic advice to ongoing policy conversations.

6.4 Driving Dynamic Change

In 2010, Doug Lemov published a book called *Teach like a Champion*. It has been estimated that one-quarter of the teacher population in the United States subsequently read the book or were exposed to techniques in it. The book rapidly gained influence in many countries around the world, including Brazil, India and China. It soon appeared in a second edition. Lemov wrote the book after he had spent a great deal of time seeking to understand how teachers in public schools that were attended mostly by disadvantaged children were nonetheless able to work with those children and help them attain relatively high scores compared with children in other public schools, many of whom experienced much less disadvantage (Lemov 2010). Lemov was motivated to understand what made these teachers effective because he was on the leadership team of Uncommon Schools, a chain of charter schools first established in Massachusetts, which subsequently spread to other states. As public schools of choice, charter schools can maintain financial viability only by attracting and keeping students who would otherwise attend their local public schools.

This is a story of dynamic change. Doug Lemov has played a part in creating that change, but I do not think of him as a policy entrepreneur. In 1989, Minnesota was the first state in the United States to introduce public school choice. It was a somewhat restricted school choice programme. In 1992, Minnesota followed up on this policy innovation by being the first state in the United States to introduce charter schools. Many other states subsequently adopted charter school laws – some of which were quite restrictive in the number of charter schools they allowed and the governance of them, other laws were more permissive. The policy entrepreneurship involved in promoting school choice and charter schools in Minnesota has been well-documented (Kolderie 2008; Nathan 1997; Roberts and King 1996). The activities of policy entrepreneurs in other states, who were initially inspired by the developments in Minnesota, have also been well-documented (Mintrom 2000; Vergari 2002).

It is not always the case that a policy innovation adopted in one state will spread to other states. Indeed, careful analysis has considered factors that serve to promote or inhibit the spread of such innovations (Shipan and Volden 2012). However, it is inspiring to see how dynamic change can happen. School choice and charter school laws diffused rapidly across the United States. Other countries learned from those experiments with charter schools. And the creation of those schools opened opportunities for further dynamic change, as illustrated by the actions and writings of Doug Lamov. In a world facing a lot of uncertainty and the continuous emergence challenges calling for considered policy responses, policy entrepreneurs can potentially add a lot of value. In the process, they can often catalyse dramatic processes of dynamic policy change.

6.5 Conclusion

The motivating thesis of this Element is that policy entrepreneurs play a unique role in policymaking processes. They represent a class of political actor distinguished by their efforts to introduce and drive proposals for dynamic change. As communities and countries around the world strive to achieve the UN Sustainable Development Goals, as diplomats work to avoid major natural and human-produced disasters, and as leaders at all levels work to mitigate and adapt to climate change, demand will increase for practical knowledge about how to drive and secure changes that promote good public outcomes. Significant shifts in public policy settings and related institutional structures are likely to be demanded and pursued in the years ahead. More than ever, the world needs policy entrepreneurs. Understanding their actions, why they engage in them and the conditions under which they meet with success or failure will help us make sense of our changing world.

I hope readers will leave this Element with a heightened awareness of policy entrepreneurs and their role in driving dynamic change. I hope some will be sufficiently inspired that they will, themselves, embody the role of the policy entrepreneur and collaborate with others to make the world a better place. Whenever anyone chooses to pursue a broader purpose, others pick up on their motivation and energy. They desire to get involved. The resulting social processes can be powerful. And so it becomes possible for many changes to be accomplished that might have once seemed impossible.

Bibliography

Acuto, M. 2013. 'The New Climate Leaders?' *Review of International Studies* 39(4): 835–57.

Allison, G. T. 1971. *Essence of Decision: Explaining the Cuban Missile Crisis*. Boston: Little, Brown & Company.

Anderson, S. E., R. A. DeLeo and K. Taylor. 2019. 'Policy Entrepreneurs, Legislators, and Agenda Setting: Information and Influence.' *Policy Studies Journal*, https://doi.org/10.1111/psj.12331.

Arieli, T., and N. Cohen. 2013. 'Policy Entrepreneurs and Post-Conflict Cross-Border Cooperation: A Conceptual Framework and the Israeli–Jordanian Case.' *Policy Sciences* 46 (3): 237–56.

Arnold, G., L. A. Nguyen Long and M. Gottlieb. 2017. 'Social Networks and Policy Entrepreneurship: How Relationships Shape Municipal Decision Making about High-Volume Hydraulic Fracturing.' *Policy Studies Journal* 45 (3): 414–41.

Bakir, C., and D. S. L. Jarvis. 2017. 'Contextualising the Context in Policy Entrepreneurship and Institutional Change.' *Policy and Society* 36 (4): 465–78.

Battilana, J., B. Leca and E. Boxenbaum. 2009. 'How Actors Change Institutions: Towards a Theory of Institutional Entrepreneurship.' *Academy of Management Annals* 3(1): 65–107.

Baumgartner, F. R., and B. D. Jones. 1993. *Agendas and Instability in American Politics*. Chicago: University of Chicago Press.

Baumgartner, F. R., and B. L. Leech. 1998. *Basic Interests: The Importance of Groups in Politics and in Political Science*. Princeton, NJ: Princeton University Press.

Berry, F. S., and W. D. Berry. 2018. 'Innovation and Diffusion Models in Policy Research.' In *Theories of the Policy Process*. Eds Christopher M. Weible and Paul A. Sabatier, New York: Routledge, pp. 263–308.

Berry, J. M., and C. Wilcox. 2018. *The Interest Group Society*, fifth edition. New York: Routledge.

Betsill, M., and H. Bulkeley. 2007. 'Looking Back and Thinking Ahead: A Decade of Cities and Climate Change Research.' *Local Environment* 12 (5): 447–56.

Bornstein, D., and S. Davis. 2010. *Social Entrepreneurship: What Everyone Needs to Know*. New York: Oxford University Press.

Boushey, G. 2010. *Policy Diffusion Dynamics in America*. New York: Cambridge University Press.

Boushey, G. 2012. 'Punctuated Equilibrium Theory and the Diffusion of Innovations.' *Policy Studies Journal* 40 (1): 127–46.

Brannback, M., and A. Carsrud. 2015. *Fundamentals for Becoming a Successful Entrepreneur: From Business Idea to Launch and Management*. Upper Saddle River, NJ: Pearson FT Press.

Broich, J. 2017. *Squadron: Ending the African Slave Trade*. New York: Harry N. Abrams.

Brouwer, S. 2015. *Policy Entrepreneurs in Water Governance*. New York: Springer.

Burt, R. S. 2000. 'The Network Structure of Social Capital.' *Research in Organizational Behaviour* 22: 345–423.

Cairney, P. 2013. 'Standing on the Shoulders of Giants: How Do We Combine the Insights of Multiple Theories in Public Policy Studies?' *Policy Studies Journal* 41 (1): 1–21.

Cairney, P., and M. D. Jones. 2016. 'Kingdon's Multiple Streams Approach: What Is the Empirical Impact of this Universal Theory?' *Policy Studies Journal* 44 (1): 37–58.

Carter, N., and M. Jacobs. 2014. 'Explaining Radical Policy Change: The Case of Climate Change and Energy Policy under the British Labour Government 2006–10.' *Public Administration* 92 (1): 125–41.

Casson, M. 1982. *The Entrepreneur: An Economic Theory*. London: Rowman and Littlefield.

Casson, M., and M. D. Giusta. 2007. 'Entrepreneurship and Social Capital: Analysing the Impact of Social Networks on Entrepreneurial Activity from a Rational Action Perspective.' *International Small Business Journal* 25 (3): 220–44.

Christopoulos, D., and K. Ingold. 2015. 'Exceptional or Just Well Connected? Political Entrepreneurs and Brokers in Policy Making.' *European Political Science Review* 7 (3): 475–98.

Cohen, M. D., J. G. March and J. P. Olsen. 1972. 'A Garbage Can Model of Organizational Choice.' *Administrative Science Quarterly* 17 (1): 1–25.

Collins, J. 2001. *Good to Great: Why Some Companies Make the Leap . . . and Others Don't.* New York: Harperbusiness.

Davies, S. E., and J. True. 2017. 'Norm Entrepreneurship in Foreign Policy: William Hague and the Prevention of Sexual Violence in Conflict.' *Foreign Policy Analysis* 13 (3): 701–21.

Deci, E. L., and R. M. Ryan. 1985. *Intrinsic Motivation and Self-Determination in Human Behavior*. New York: Plenum.

Derthick, M., and P. Quirk. 1985. *The Politics of Deregulation*. Washington, DC: The Brookings Institution Press.

Dewulf, A., and R. Bouwen. 2012. 'Issue Framing in Conversations for Change: Discursive Interaction Strategies for "Doing Differences".' *The Journal of Applied Behavioral Science* 48 (2): 168–93.

Dixit, A. K., and B. Nalebuff. 2008. *The Art of Strategy: A Game Theorist's Guide to Success in Business and Life*. New York: W W Norton & Company.

Dolowitz, D., and D. Marsh. 1996. 'Who Learns What from Whom: A Review of the Policy Transfer Literature.' *Political Studies* 44 (2): 343–57.

Drummond, W. J. 2010. 'Statehouse Versus Greenhouse: Have State-Level Climate Action Planners and Policy Entrepreneurs Reduced Greenhouse Gas Emissions?' *Journal of the American Planning Association* 76 (4): 413–33.

Duckworth, A. 2016. *Grit: The Power of Passion and Perseverance*. New York: Scribner.

Dudley, G. 2013. 'Why Do Ideas Succeed and Fail Over Time?: The Role of Narratives in Policy Windows and the Case of the London Congestion Charge.' *Journal of European Public Policy* 20 (8): 1139–56.

Dye, T. R. 1976. *Who's Running America?: Institutional Leadership in the United States*. Englewood Cliffs, NJ: Prentice-Hall.

Dye, T. R. 2014. *Who's Running America? The Obama Reign*, eighth edition. New York: Routledge.

Easton, D. 1969. 'The New Revolution in Political Science.' *American Political Science Review* 63 (4): 1051–61.

Ericsson, K. A., M. J. Prietula and E. T. Cokely. 2007. 'The Making of an Expert.' *Harvard Business Review* 85: 115–21.

Evans, P. B., D. Rueschemeyer and T. Skocpol (eds). 1985. *Bringing the State Back In*. New York: Cambridge University Press.

Faling, M., R. Biesbroek, S. Karlsson-Vinkhuyzen and K. Termeer. 2018. 'Policy Entrepreneurship across Boundaries: A Systematic Literature Review.' *Journal of Public Policy* 39 (2): 393–422.

Falleti, T. G. 2010. 'Infiltrating the State: The Evolution of Health Care Reforms in Brazil, 1964–1988.' In *Explaining Institutional Change: Ambiguity, Agency, and Power*. Eds J. Mahoney and K. A. Thelen, New York: Cambridge University Press, pp. 38–62.

Feldman, M. S., and A. M. Khademian. 2002. 'To Manage Is to Govern.' *Public Administration Review* 62: 541–55.

Feiock, R. C., and J. Bae. 2011. 'Politics, Institutions and Entrepreneurship: City Decisions Leading to inventoried GHG Emissions.' *Carbon Management* 2 (4): 443–53.

Fisher R, W. L. Ury and B. Patton. 1991. *Getting to YES: Negotiating Agreement without Giving In*, second edition. Hammondsworth: Penguin.

Frisch-Aviram, N., N. Cohen and I. Beeri. 2018. 'Low-Level Bureaucrats, Local Government Regimes and Policy Entrepreneurship.' *Policy Sciences* 51 (1): 39–57.

Frisch-Aviram, N., N. Cohen and I. Beeri. 2019. 'Wind(ow) of Change: A Systematic Review of Policy Entrepreneurship Characteristics and Strategies.' *Policy Studies Journal*, https://doi.org/10.1111/psj.12339.

Geva-May, I. 2004. 'Riding the Wave of Opportunity: Termination in Public Policy.' *Journal of Public Administration Research and Theory* 14: 309–33.

Glick, H. R., and S. P. Hays. 1991. 'Innovation and Reinvention in State Policymaking: Theory and the Evolution of Living Will Laws.' *The Journal of Politics* 53 (3): 835–50.

Goldfinch, S., and P. 't Hart. 2003. 'Leadership and Institutional Reform: Engineering Macroeconomic Policy Change in Australia.' *Governance* 16: 235–70.

Hajime, S. 1999. 'The Advocacy Coalition Framework and the Policy Process Analysis: The Case of Smoking Control in Japan.' *Policy Studies Journal* 27: 28–44.

Hall, P. A., and R. C. Taylor. 1996. 'Political Science and the Three New Institutionalisms.' *Political Studies* 44 (5): 936–57.

Hammond, D. R. 2013. 'Policy Entrepreneurship in China's Response to Urban Poverty.' *Policy Studies Journal* 41 (1): 119–46.

He, A. J. 2018. 'Manoeuvring within a Fragmented Bureaucracy: Policy Entrepreneurship in China's Local Healthcare Reform'. *The China Quarterly* 236: 1088–110.

Heifetz, R. A. 1994. *Leadership without Easy Answers*. Cambridge, MA: Harvard University Press.

Henig, J. R. 2008. *Spin Cycle: How Research Gets Used in Policy Debates – The Case of Charter Schools*. New York: Russell Sage Foundation.

Herweg, N., N. Zahariadis and R. Zohlnhöfer. 2018. 'The Multiple Streams Framework: Foundations, Refinements, and Empirical Applications.' Chapter 1 in *Theories of the Policy Process*, fourth edition. Eds C. Weible and P. A. Sabatier. New York: Routledge, pp. 17–54.

Howlett, M., and M. Ramesh. 2016. 'Achilles' Heels of Governance: Critical Capacity Deficits and Their Role in Governance Failures.' *Regulation and Governance* 10 (4): 301–13.

Huitema, D., L. Lebel and S. Meijerink. 2011. 'The Strategies of Policy Entrepreneurs in Water Transitions around the World.' *Water Policy* 13 (5): 717–33.

Jobs, S. 1997. 'Here's to the Crazy Ones.' Narrative on Apple's Think Different commercial. www.youtube.com/watch?v=-z4NS2zdrZc, last accessed 19 September 2019.

John, P. 1999. 'Ideas and Interests; Agendas and Implementation: An Evolutionary Explanation of Policy Change in British Local Government Finance.' *British Journal of Politics and International Relations* 1: 39–62.

John, P. 2003. 'Is There Life after Policy Streams, Advocacy Coalitions, and Punctuations?: Using Evolutionary Theory to Explain Policy Change.' *Policy Studies Journal* 31: 481–98.

Kalafatis, S. E., and M. C. Lemos. 2017. 'The Emergence of Climate Change Policy Entrepreneurs in Urban Regions.' *Regional Environmental Change* 17 (6): 1791–9.

Kalil, T. 2017. 'Policy Entrepreneurship at the White House: Getting Things Done in Large Organizations.' *Innovations: Technology, Governance, Globalization* 11 (3–4): 4–21.

Kammerer, M., and C. Namhata. 2018. 'What Drives the Adoption of Climate Change Mitigation Policy? A Dynamic Network Approach to Policy Diffusion.' *Policy Sciences* 51 (4): 477–513.

Kern, K., and H. Bulkeley. 2009. 'Cities, Europeanization and Multi-Level Governance: Governing Climate Change through Transnational Municipal Networks.' *Journal of Common Market Studies* 47 (2): 309–32.

Kingdon, J. W. 1984 [2011]. *Agendas, Alternatives, and Public Policies*, third edition. Boston: Little, Brown & Company.

Kirkpatrick, K. J., and Stoutenborough, J. W. 2018. 'Strategy, Narratives, and Reading the Public: Developing a Micro-Level Theory of Political Strategies within the Narrative Policy Framework.' *Policy Studies Journal* 46 (4): 949–77.

Kirzner, I. M. 1973. 'Entrepreneurship and the Equilibrating Process.' In *Competition and Entrepreneurship*. Ed. I. M. Kirzner, Chicago: Mifflin.

Kirzner, I. M. 1997. 'Entrepreneurial Discovery and the Competitive Market Process: An Austrian Approach.' *Journal of Economic Literature* 35 (1): 60–85.

Klein, J. 2006. *For All These Rights: Business, Labor, and the Shaping of America's Public-Private Welfare State*. Princeton, NJ: Princeton University Press.

Knoke, D. 1990. 'Networks of Political Action: Toward Theory Construction.' *Social Forces* 68 (4): 1041–63.

Knott, J. H., and D. McCarthy. 2007. 'Policy Venture Capital: Foundations, Government Partnerships, and Child Care Programs.' *Administration and Society* 39 (3): 319–53.

Kolderie, T. 2008. 'How the idea of 'Chartering' Schools Came About.' *Minnesota Journal* 5 (June): 5–6.

Kotter, J. 1996. *Leading Change*. Boston: Harvard Business School Press.

Lemov, D. 2010. *Teach like a Champion: 49 Techniques that Put Students on the Path to College (K-12)*, second edition. New York: John Wiley and Sons.

Levin, M. A., and M. B. Sanger. 1994. *Making Government Work: How Entrepreneurial Executives Turn Bright Ideas into Real Results*. San Francisco: Jossey-Bass.

Lindblom, C. E., 1959. 'The Science of Muddling Through.' *Public Administration Review* 19 (2): 79–88.

Lindblom, C. E. 1968. The Policy-Making Process. Englewood Cliffs, NJ: Prentice-Hall.

Lindblom, C. E. 1979. 'Still Muddling, Not Yet Through.' *Public Administration Review* 39 (6): 517–26.

Litfin, K. T. 2000. 'Advocacy Coalitions along the Domestic-Foreign Frontier: Globalization and Canadian Climate Change Policy.' *Policy Studies Journal* 28: 236–52.

Lubell, M., J. Scholz, R. Berardo and G. Robbins. 2012. 'Testing Policy Theory with Statistical Models of Networks.' *Policy Studies Journal* 40 (3): 351–74.

Mack, W. R., D. Green and A. Vedlitz. 2008. 'Innovation and Implementation in the Public Sector: An Examination of Public Entrepreneurship.' *Review of Policy Research* 25 (3): 233–52.

Majone, G. 1996. 'Public Policy and Administration: Ideas, Interests and Institutions.' In *A New Handbook of Political Science*. Ed. Robert E. Goodin and Hans-Dieter Klingemann, New York: Oxford University Press, pp. 610–27.

March, J. G., and J. P. Olsen. 1983. 'The New Institutionalism: Organizational Factors in Political Life.' *American Political Science Review* 78 (3): 734–49.

March, J. G., and J. P. Olsen. 1989. *Rediscovering Institutions: The Organizational Basis of Politics*. New York: Free Press.

Margolit, Angela, and Caryn Kopp (eds). (2019). *Lessons beyond the Obvious: The Entrepreneur's Handbook*. Savannah, GA: Angela Margolit.

Marsh, D. and J. C. Sharman. 2009. 'Policy Diffusion and Policy Transfer.' *Policy Studies* 30 (3): 269–88.

Mazzeo, M., P. E. Oyer and S. J. Schaefer. 2014. *The Roadside MBA: Backroad Lessons for Entrepreneurs, Executives and Small Business Owners*. New York: Business Plus.

McCubbins, M. D., and T. Schwartz. 1984. 'Congressional Oversight Overlooked: Police Patrols Versus Fire Alarms.' *American Journal of Political Science* 28 (1): 165–79.

McGranahan, G., D. Balk and B. Anderson. 2007. 'The Rising Tide: Assessing the Risks of Climate Change and Human Settlements in Low Elevation Coastal Zones.' *Environment and Urbanization* 19 (1): 17–37.

Meier, D. 2002. *The Power of Their Ideas: Lessons for America from a Small School in Harlem*. Boston: Beacon Press.

Meier, K., and L. J. O'Toole. 2001. 'Managerial Strategies and Behaviour in Networks: A Model with Evidence from US Public Administration.' *Journal of Public Administration Research and Theory* 11 (3): 271–94.

Meijerink, S. 2005. 'Understanding Policy Stability and Change: The Interplay of Advocacy Coalitions and Epistemic Communities, Windows of Opportunity, and Dutch Coastal Flooding Policy 1945–2003.' *Journal of European Public Policy* 12: 1060–77.

Melvern, L. 2013. 'Aloisea Inyumba: Politician Who Played a Key Role in the Rebuilding of Rwanda' *The Independent*, 8 March, www.independent.co.uk/news/obituaries/aloisea-inyumba-politician-who-played-a-key-role-in-the-rebuilding-of-rwanda-8527166.html, last accessed 28 February 2019.

Metaxas, E. 2007. *Amazing Grace: William Wilberforce and the Heroic Campaign to End Slavery*. New York: HarperCollins.

Mettler, S. 1998. *Dividing Citizens: Gender and Federalism in New Deal Public Policy*. Ithaca, NY: Cornell University Press.

Mettler, S. 2007. *Soldiers to Citizens: The G.I. Bill and the Making of the Greatest Generation*. New York: Oxford University Press.

Mills, C. W. 1956. *The Power Elite*. New York: Oxford University Press.

Mintrom, M. 1997a. 'The State-Local Nexus in Policy Innovation Diffusion: The Case of School Choice.' *Publius: The Journal of Federalism* 27: 41–60.

Mintrom, M. 1997b. 'Policy Entrepreneurs and the Diffusion of Innovation.' *American Journal of Political Science* 41: 738–70.

Mintrom, M. 2000. *Policy Entrepreneurs and School Choice*. Washington, DC: Georgetown University Press.

Mintrom, M. 2003. *People Skills for Policy Analysts*. Washington, DC: Georgetown University Press.

Mintrom, M. 2013. 'Policy Entrepreneurs and Controversial Science: Governing Human Embryonic Stem Cell Research.' *Journal of European Public Policy* 20: 442–57.

Mintrom, M. 2014 'Creating Cultures of Excellence: Strategies and Outcomes.' *Cogent Education* 1 (1): 1–14.

Mintrom, M. 2015. 'Policy Entrepreneurs and Morality Politics: Learning from Failure and Success.' Chapter 8 in *Entrepreneurship in the Polis: Contested Entrepreneurs and Dynamics of Change in Diverse Contexts*. Eds

I. Narbutaite Aflaki, L. Miles and E. Petridou, Farnham: Ashgate Publishing, pp. 103–18.

Mintrom, M., and J. Luetjens. 2017. 'Policy Entrepreneurs and Problem Framing: The Case of Climate Change.' *Environment and Planning C: Politics and Space* 35 (8): 1362–77.

Mintrom, M., and P. Norman. 2009. 'Policy Entrepreneurship and Policy Change.' *Policy Studies Journal* 37: 649–67.

Mintrom, M., C. Salisbury and J. Luetjens. 2014. 'Policy Entrepreneurs and the Promotion of Australian State Knowledge Economies.' *Australian Journal of Political Science* 49 (3): 423–38.

Mintrom, M., and M. Thomas. 2018. 'Policy Entrepreneurs and Collaborative Action: Pursuit of the Sustainable Development Goals.' *International Journal of Entrepreneurial Venturing* 10 (2): 153–71.

Mintrom, M., and S. Vergari. 1996. 'Advocacy Coalitions, Policy Entrepreneurs, and Policy Change.' *Policy Studies Journal* 24: 420–34.

Mintrom, M., and S. Vergari. 1998. 'Policy Networks and Innovation Diffusion: The Case of State Education Reforms.' *Journal of Politics* 60: 126–48.

Mintrom, M., and S. Vergari. 2009. 'Foundation Engagement in Education Policymaking: Assessing Philanthropic Support of School Choice initiatives.' In *Foundations and Public Policy: Leveraging Philanthropic Dollars, Knowledge, and Networks for Greater Impact*. Ed. J. M. Ferris, New York: The Foundation Center, pp.243–78.

Moe, T. M. (ed.). 1995. *Private Vouchers*. Stanford, CA: Hoover Institution Press.

Mohr, L. B. 1969. 'Determinants of Innovation in Organizations.' *American Political Science Review* 63 (1): 111–26.

Mooney, C. Z., and M. H. Lee. 1995. 'Legislative Morality in the American States: The Case of pre-Roe Abortion Regulation Reform.' *American Journal of Political Science* 39 (3): 599–627.

Munyaneza, J. 2012. 'The Passing of an Icon.' *New Times*, 7 December, www.newtimes.co.rw/section/read/60545, last accessed 28 February 2019.

Narbutaite Aflaki, I., L. Miles and E. Petridou (eds). 2015. *Entrepreneurship in the Polis: Contested Entrepreneurs and Dynamics of Change in Diverse Contexts*. Farnham: Ashgate Publishing.

Nathan, J. 1997. *Charter Schools: Creating Hope and Opportunity for American Education*. San Francisco: Jossey-Bass Inc.

Navot, D., and N. Cohen. 2015. 'How Policy Entrepreneurs Reduce Corruption in Israel.' *Governance* 28 (1): 61–76.

Nelson, B. 1984. *Making an Issue of Child Abuse*. Chicago: University of Chicago Press.

North, D. C. 1981. *Structure and Change in Economic History.* New York: Norton.

North, D. C. 1990. *Institutions, Institutional Change, and Economic Performance.* New York: Cambridge University Press.

Oborn, E., M. Barrett and M. Exworthy. 2011. 'Policy Entrepreneurship in the Development of Public Sector Strategy: The Case of London Health Reform.' *Public Administration* 89 (2): 325–44.

Oliver, T. R., and P. Paul-Shaheen. 1997. 'Translating Ideas into Actions: Entrepreneurial Leadership in State Health Care Reforms.' *Journal of Health Politics, Policy and Law* 22 (3): 721–89.

Peters, B. G. 1994. 'Agenda-setting in the European Community.' *Journal of European Public Policy* 1 (1): 9–26.

Petridou, E. 2014. 'Theories of the Policy Process: Contemporary Scholarship and Future Directions.' *Policy Studies Journal* 42: S12–S32.

Petridou, E. 2016. *Political Entrepreneurship in Swedish: Towards a (Re) Theorization of Entrepreneurial Agency.* A doctoral thesis. Mid Sweden University, Östersund.

Polsby, N. W. 1985. *Political Innovation in America: The Politics of Policy Initiation.* New Haven, CT: Yale University Press.

Powell, W. W., and P. J. DiMaggio (eds). 1991. *The New Institutionalism in Organizational Analysis.* Chicago: University of Chicago Press.

Provost, C. 2003. 'State Attorneys General, Entrepreneurship, and Consumer Protection in the New Federalism.' *Publius: The Journal of Federalism* 33 (2): 37–53.

Quinn, R. E. 2000. *Change the World: How Ordinary People Can Achieve Extraordinary Results.* San Francisco: Jossey-Bass.

Quinn, R. W., and R. E. Quinn. 2009. *Lift: Becoming a Positive Force in Any Situation.* San Francisco: Berrett-Koehler Publishers.

Rabe, B. G. 2004. *Statehouse and Greenhouse: The Emerging Politics of American Climate Change Policy.* Washington, DC: Brookings Institution Press.

Roberts, N. C., and P. J. King. 1991. 'Policy Entrepreneurs: Their Activity Structure and Function in the Policy Process.' *Journal of Public Administration Research and Theory* 1 (2): 147–75.

Roberts, N. C., and P. J. King. 1996. *Transforming Public Policy: Dynamics of Policy Entrepreneurship and Innovation.* San Francisco: Jossey-Bass.

Rochefort, D. A., and R. W. Cobb (eds). 1994. *The Politics of Problem Definition: Shaping the Policy Agenda.* Lawrence: University Press of Kansas.

Rogers, E. 1962 [2003]. *Diffusion of Innovation,* fifth edition. New York: Basic Books.

Sabatier, P. A. 1988. 'An Advocacy Coalition Framework of Policy Change and the Role of Policy-Oriented Learning Therein.' *Policy Sciences* 21 (2–3): 129–68.

Sabatier, P. A., and H. Jenkins-Smith. 1993. *Policy Change and Learning: An Advocacy Coalition Approach*. Boulder, CO: Westview Press.

Scharpf, F. 1997. *Games Real Actors Play. Actor-Centered Institutionalism in Policy Research*. Boulder, CO: Westview Press.

Schattschneider, E. E. 1960. *The Semisovereign People: A Realist's View of Democracy in America*. New York: Holt, Rinehart and Winston.

Schneider, A. L., and H. Ingram. 1993. *Policy Design for Democracy*. Lawrence: University Press of Kansas.

Schneider, M., and P. Teske. 1992. 'Toward a Theory of the Political Entrepreneur: Evidence from Local Government.' *American Political Science Review* 86 (3): 737–47.

Schneider, M., and P. Teske, with M. Mintrom. 1995. *Public Entrepreneurs: Agents for Change in American Government*. Princeton, NJ: Princeton University Press.

Schön, D., and M. Rein. 1994. *Frame Reflection: Toward the Resolution of Intractable Policy Controversies*. New York: Basic Books.

Schreurs, M. A. 2008. 'From the Bottom Up: Local and Subnational Climate Change Politics.' *The Journal of Environment and Development* 17 (4): 343–55.

Schumpeter, J. A. 1934. *The Theory of Economic Development*, trans. Redvers Opie. Cambridge, MA: Harvard University Press.

Sheingate, A. D. 2003. 'Political Entrepreneurship, Institutional Change, and American Political Development.' *Studies in American Political Development* 17 (2): 185–203.

Shipan, C. R., and C. Volden. 2008. 'The Mechanisms of Policy Diffusion.' *American Journal of Political Science* 52 (4): 840–57.

Shipan, C. R., and C. Volden. 2012. 'Policy Diffusion: Seven Lessons for Scholars and Practitioners.' *Public Administration Review* 72 (6): 788–96.

Shpaizman, I., O. Swed and A. Pedahzur. 2016. 'Policy Change Inch by Inch: Policy Entrepreneurs in the Holy Basin of Jerusalem.' *Public Administration* 94 (4): 1042–58.

Simon, H. A. 1947. *Administrative Behavior: A Study of Decision-Making Processes in Administrative Organization*. New York, Macmillan Co.

Stone, D. A. 1997. *Policy Paradox: The Art of Political Decision Making*. New York: W W Norton.

Sugiyama, N. B. 2011. 'Bottom-Up Policy Diffusion: National Emulation of a Conditional Cash Transfer Program in Brazil.' *Publius: The Journal of Federalism* 42 (1): 25–51.

Teets, J. C. 2015. 'The Politics of Innovation in China: Local Officials as Policy Entrepreneurs.' *Issues and Studies* 51 (2): 79–109.

Teske, P. (ed.). 2004. *Regulation in the States*. Washington, DC: Brookings Institution Press.

True, J., and M. Mintrom. 2001. 'Transnational Networks and Policy Diffusion: The Case of Gender Mainstreaming.' *International Studies Quarterly* 45 (1): 27–57.

True, J. L. 2000. 'Avalanches and Incrementalism.' *The American Review of Public Administration* 30: 3–18.

Truman, H. S. 1948. Quotation sourced from Harry S Truman Quotes. BrainyQuote.com, BrainyMedia Inc, 2019. www.brainyquote.com/quotes/ harry_s_truman_109615, last accessed 17 September 2019.

Tyack, D. B. 1974. *The One Best System: A History of American Urban Education*. Cambridge, MA: Harvard University Press.

Tyack D. B., and L. Cuban. 1995. *Tinkering Toward Utopia*. Cambridge, MA: Harvard University Press.

van de Ven, A. H. 1986. 'Central Problems in the Management of Innovation.' *Management Science* 32 (5): 590–607.

Vergari, S. 1999. 'Charter Schools: A Primer on the Issues.' *Education and Urban Society* 31 (4): 389–405.

Vergari, S. (ed.). 2002. *The Charter School Landscape*. Pittsburgh, PA: University of Pittsburgh Press.

Victor, D. G., J. C. House and S. Joy. 2005. 'A Madisonian Approach to Climate Policy.' *Science* 309 (5742): 1820–1.

Walker, J. L. 1969. 'The Diffusion of Innovations among the American States.' *American Political Science Review* 63 (3): 880–99.

Weible, C. M., and P. Cairney. 2018. 'Practical Lessons from Policy Theories.' *Policy and Politics* 46 (2): 183–97.

Weible, C. M., and P. A. Sabatier, 2009. 'Coalitions, Science, and Belief Change: Comparing Adversarial and Collaborative Policy Subsystems.' *Policy Studies Journal* 37 (2): 195–212.

Yi, H., and J. T. Scholz. 2015. 'Policy Networks in Complex Governance Subsystems.' *Policy Studies Journal* 44 (3): 1–32.

Acknowledgements

As the content of this Element shows, research on policy entrepreneurs has flourished over the past three decades. Exciting possibilities exist for future research, which promises to enhance our understandings of contemporary political processes everywhere, from the local level to the global. I am grateful to Michael Howlett and M. Ramesh for encouraging me to produce this Cambridge Element, and to Andrew Gunn and three anonymous referees for their advice regarding ways to improve it. I am privileged to enjoy a family life that is highly conducive to thinking, research and writing. I extend unending thanks to my Monash University colleague and partner, Jacqui True, and our sons, Seamus and Hugo, for being so supportive of my career, and especially for their support as I completed this manuscript. My interest in policy entrepreneurs developed when I was studying for my PhD in political science at the State University of New York at Stony Brook. I am indebted to Mark Schneider and Paul Teske for the rich research culture they established around them and the guidance and support they gave me during those years. Our co-authored book, *Public Entrepreneurs: Agents for Change in American Government* (1995), and my subsequent book, *Policy Entrepreneurs and School Choice* (2000), attest to the strength of that collaborative culture. Since then, my collaborations and conversations with many people in many places have allowed me to advance my understanding of policy entrepreneurs and how they promote dynamic change. I especially wish to thank Stijn Brouwer, Nissim Cohen, Andrew Gunn, Dave Huitema, Stephan Kuhnert, Joannah Luetjens, Phillipa Norman, Evangelia Petridou, Chris Salisbury, Madeline Thomas and Sandra Vergari. I completed this manuscript at the Australia and New Zealand School of Government in Melbourne. The school provided a highly supportive and intellectually stimulating research environment. I am grateful to Ken Smith, dean and CEO, for encouraging continuous, deeply engaged discussions between researchers and government leaders about contemporary issues in public policy and public management. I also appreciate the work of Madeline Thomas who served as my colleague at the Australia and New Zealand School of Government, and who provided excellent research support and editorial assistance throughout the development of this manuscript.

Cambridge Elements

Public Policy

M. Ramesh
National University of Singapore (NUS)

M. Ramesh is UNESCO Chair on Social Policy Design at the Lee Kuan Yew School of Public Policy, NUS. His research focuses on governance and social policy in East and Southeast Asia, in addition to public policy institutions and processes. He has published extensively in reputed international journals. He is Co-editor of Policy and Society and Policy Design and Practice.

Michael Howlett
Simon Fraser University, British Colombia

Michael Howlett is Burnaby Mountain Professor and Canada Research Chair (Tier 1) in the Department of Political Science, Simon Fraser University. He specialises in public policy analysis, and resource and environmental policy. He is currently editor-in-chief of *Policy Sciences* and co-editor of the *Journal of Comparative Policy Analysis; Policy and Society* and *Policy Design and Practice.*

Xun WU
Hong Kong University of Science and Technology

Xun WU is Professor and Head of the Division of Public Policy at the Hong Kong University of Science and Technology. He is a policy scientist whose research interests include policy innovations, water resource management and health policy reform. He has been involved extensively in consultancy and executive education, his work involving consultations for the World Bank and UNEP.

Judith Clifton
University of Cantabria

Judith Clifton is Professor of Economics at the University of Cantabria, Spain. She has published in leading policy journals and is editor-in-chief of the *Journal of Economic Policy Reform.* Most recently, her research enquires how emerging technologies can transform public administration, a forward-looking cutting-edge project which received €3.5 million funding from the Horizon2020 programme.

Eduardo Araral
National University of Singapore (NUS)

Eduardo Araral is widely published in various journals and books and has presented in forty conferences. He is currently Co-Director of the Institute of Water Policy at the Lee Kuan Yew School of Public Policy, NUS and is a member of the editorial board of *Journal of Public Administration Research and Theory* and the board of the Public Management Research Association.

About the series

Elements in Public Policy is a concise and authoritative collection of assessments of the state of the art and future research directions in public policy research, as well as substantive new research on key topics. Edited by leading scholars in the field, the series is an ideal medium for reflecting on and advancing the understanding of critical issues in the public sphere. Collectively, it provides a forum for broad and diverse coverage of all major topics in the field while integrating different disciplinary and methodological approaches.

Cambridge Elements ☰

Public Policy

Printed in the United States
By Bookmasters